Here's To You, Charlie Brown

Selected Cartoons
from YOU CAN'T WIN
CHARLIE BROWN VOL II

Charles M. Schulz

CORONET BOOKS
Hodder Fawcett, London

First published by Fawcett Publications Inc.,
New York, 1969

Coronet edition 1969
Eighth impression 1977

Printed in Great Britain for Hodder Fawcett Ltd.,
Mill Road, Dunton Green, Sevenoaks, Kent
(Editorial Office: 47 Bedford Square, London WC1 3DP)
by C. Nicholls & Company Ltd
The Philips Park Press, Manchester

ISBN 0 340 10595 X

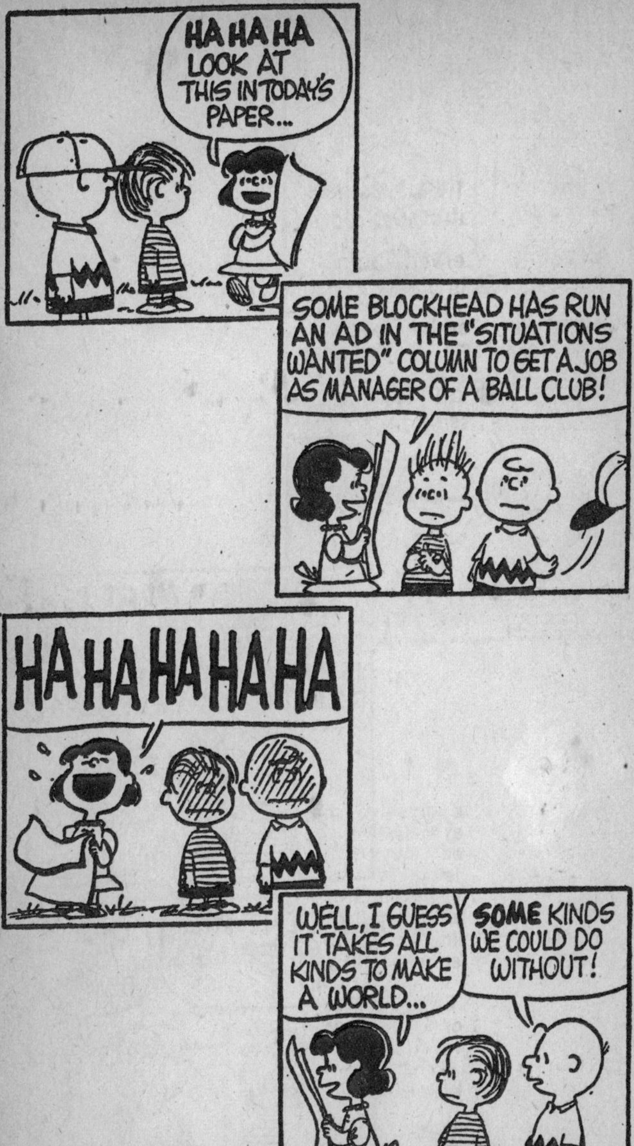
HA HA HA
LOOK AT THIS IN TODAY'S PAPER...
SOME BLOCKHEAD HAS RUN AN AD IN THE "SITUATIONS WANTED" COLUMN TO GET A JOB AS MANAGER OF A BALL CLUB!
HA HA HA HA HA HA
WELL, I GUESS IT TAKES ALL KINDS TO MAKE A WORLD...
SOME KINDS WE COULD DO WITHOUT!

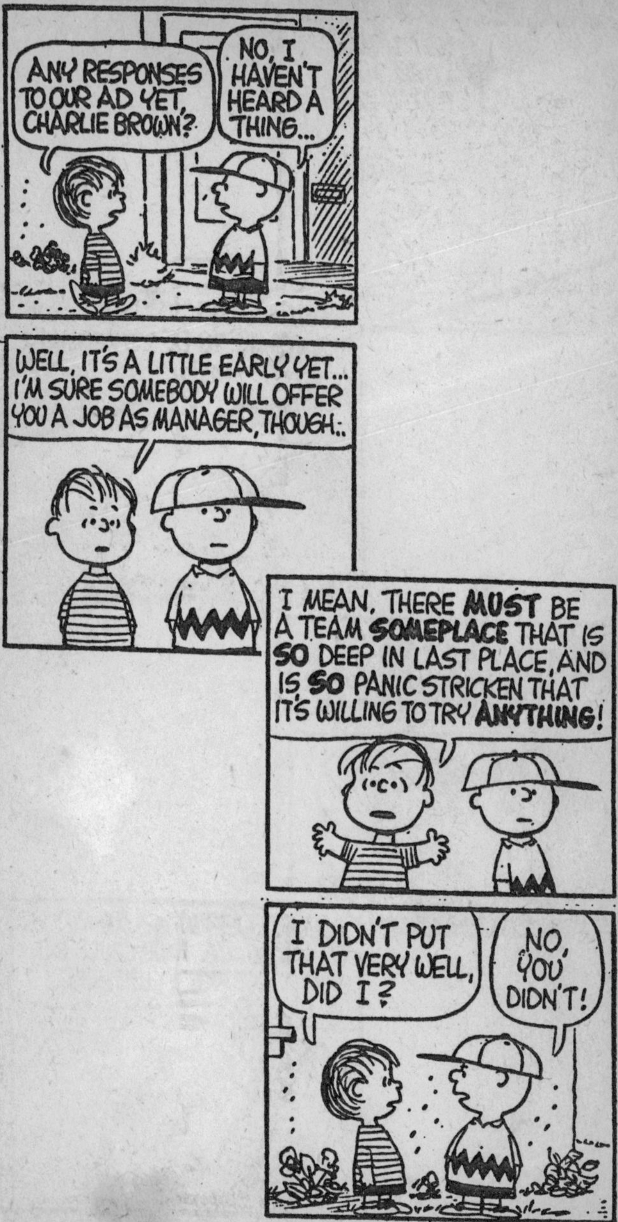
ANY RESPONSES TO OUR AD YET, CHARLIE BROWN?
NO, I HAVEN'T HEARD A THING...
WELL, IT'S A LITTLE EARLY YET... I'M SURE SOMEBODY WILL OFFER YOU A JOB AS MANAGER, THOUGH..
I MEAN, THERE MUST BE A TEAM SOMEPLACE THAT IS SO DEEP IN LAST PLACE, AND IS SO PANIC STRICKEN THAT IT'S WILLING TO TRY ANYTHING!
I DIDN'T PUT THAT VERY WELL, DID I?
NO, YOU DIDN'T!

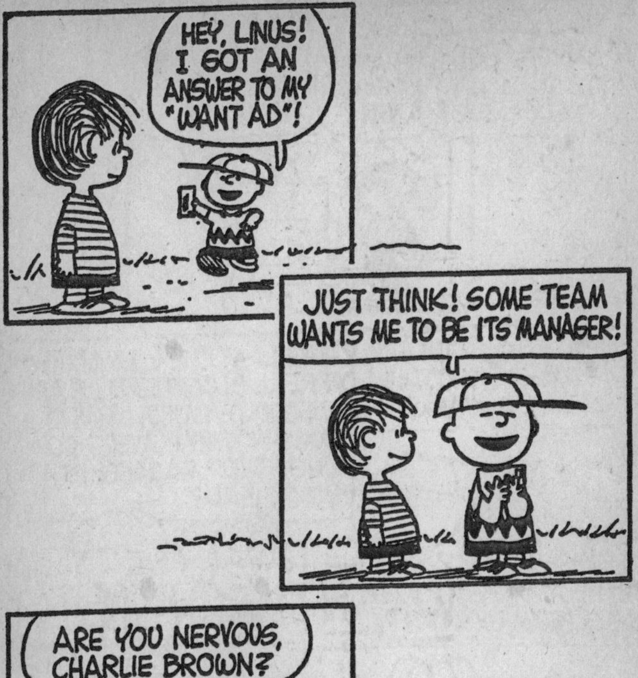
HEY, LINUS! I GOT AN ANSWER TO MY "WANT AD"!
JUST THINK! SOME TEAM WANTS ME TO BE ITS MANAGER!
ARE YOU NERVOUS, CHARLIE BROWN?
NERVOUS? WHAT MAKES YOU THINK I'M NERVOUS?

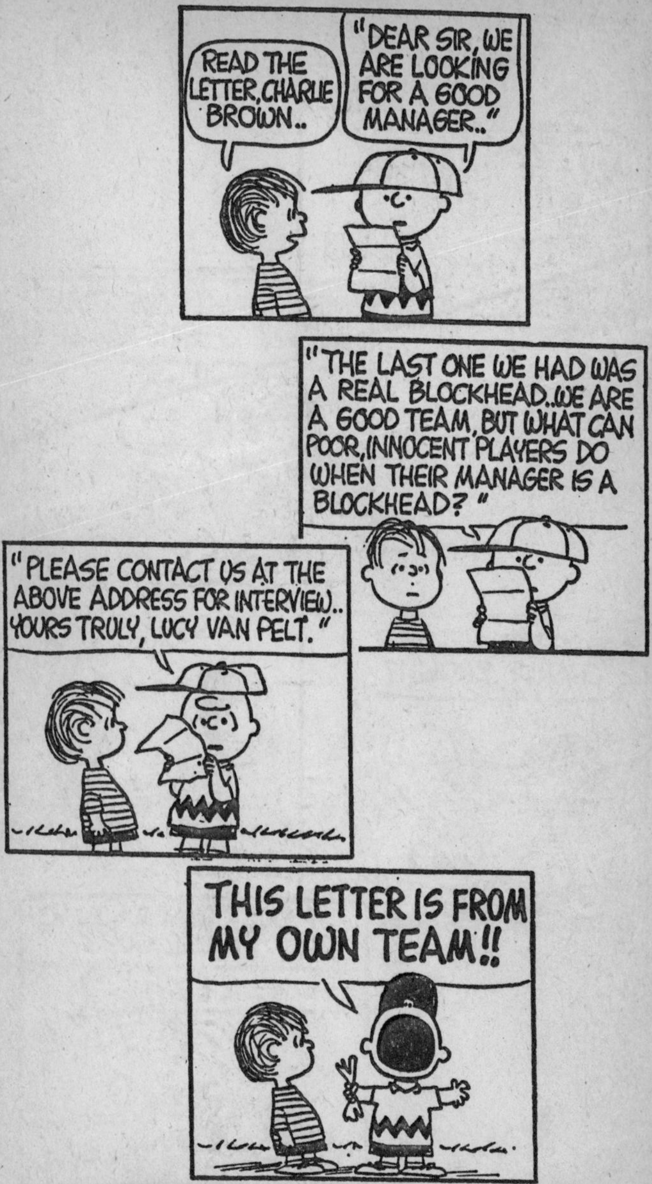
READ THE LETTER, CHARLIE BROWN..
"DEAR SIR, WE ARE LOOKING FOR A GOOD MANAGER.."
"THE LAST ONE WE HAD WAS A REAL BLOCKHEAD..WE ARE A GOOD TEAM, BUT WHAT CAN POOR, INNOCENT PLAYERS DO WHEN THEIR MANAGER IS A BLOCKHEAD?"
"PLEASE CONTACT US AT THE ABOVE ADDRESS FOR INTERVIEW.. YOURS TRULY, LUCY VAN PELT."
THIS LETTER IS FROM MY OWN TEAM!!

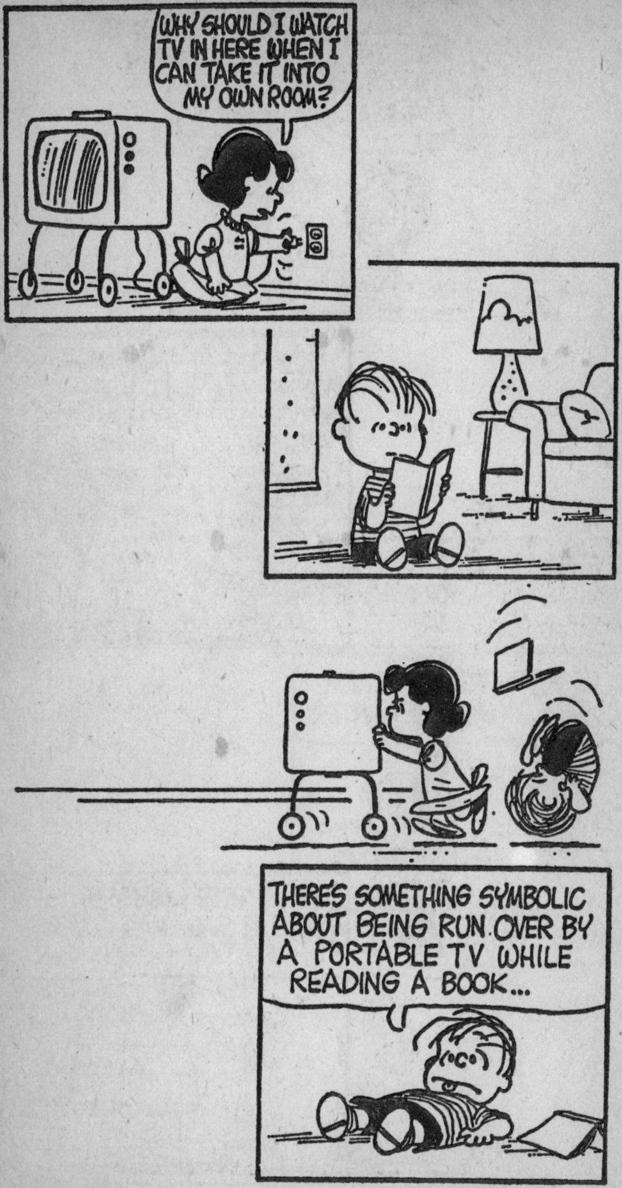
WHY SHOULD I WATCH TV IN HERE WHEN I CAN TAKE IT INTO MY OWN ROOM?
THERE'S SOMETHING SYMBOLIC ABOUT BEING RUN OVER BY A PORTABLE TV WHILE READING A BOOK...

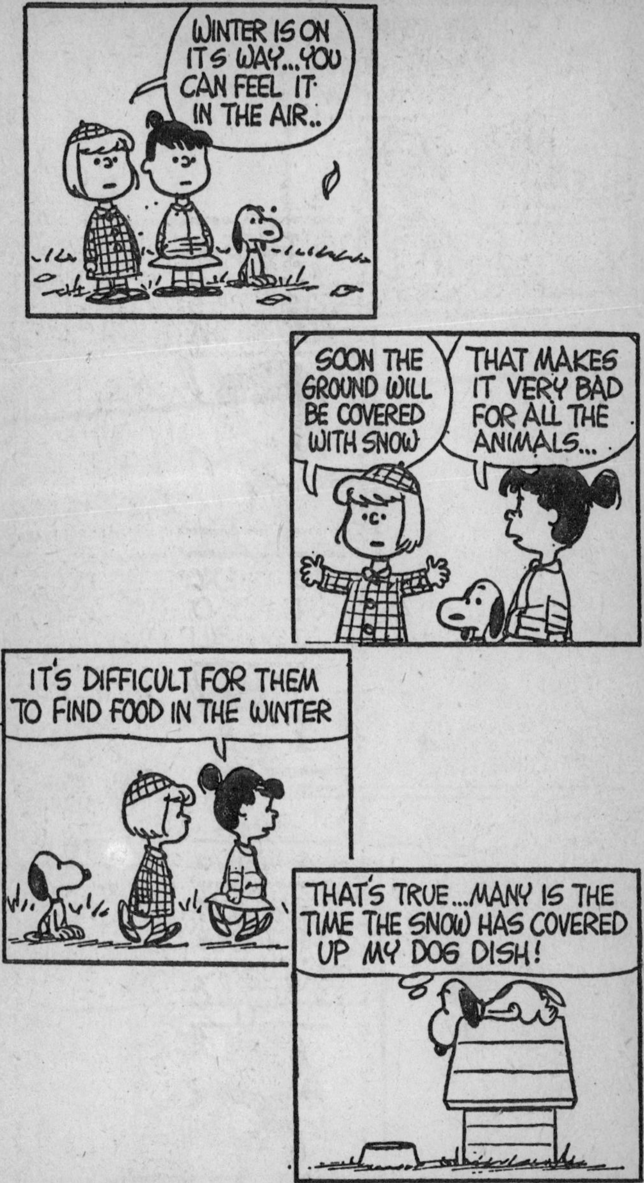
WINTER IS ON ITS WAY...YOU CAN FEEL IT IN THE AIR..
SOON THE GROUND WILL BE COVERED WITH SNOW
THAT MAKES IT VERY BAD FOR ALL THE ANIMALS...
IT'S DIFFICULT FOR THEM TO FIND FOOD IN THE WINTER
THAT'S TRUE...MANY IS THE TIME THE SNOW HAS COVERED UP MY DOG DISH!

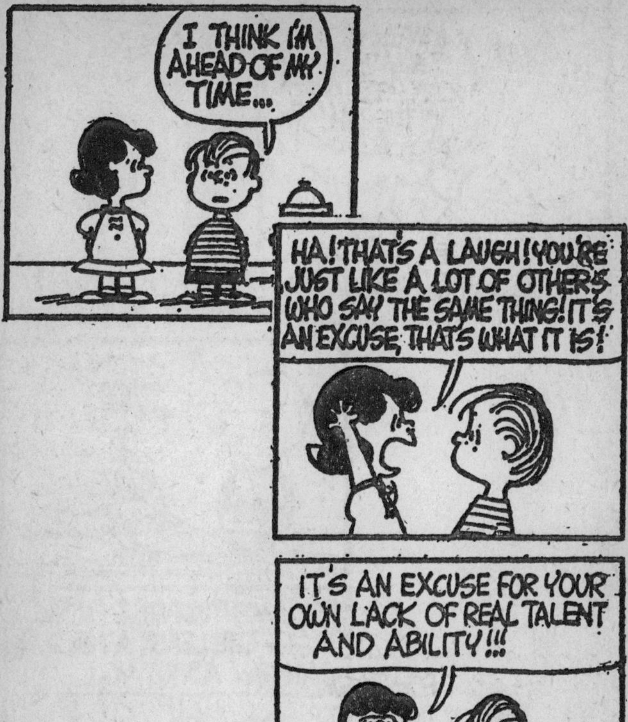
I THINK I'M AHEAD OF MY TIME...
HA! THAT'S A LAUGH! YOU'RE JUST LIKE A LOT OF OTHERS WHO SAY THE SAME THING! IT'S AN EXCUSE, THAT'S WHAT IT IS!
IT'S AN EXCUSE FOR YOUR OWN LACK OF REAL TALENT AND ABILITY!!!
I WAS SUPPOSED TO MEET CHARLIE BROWN HERE AT TWO O'CLOCK, BUT I THINK I'M AHEAD OF MY TIME..

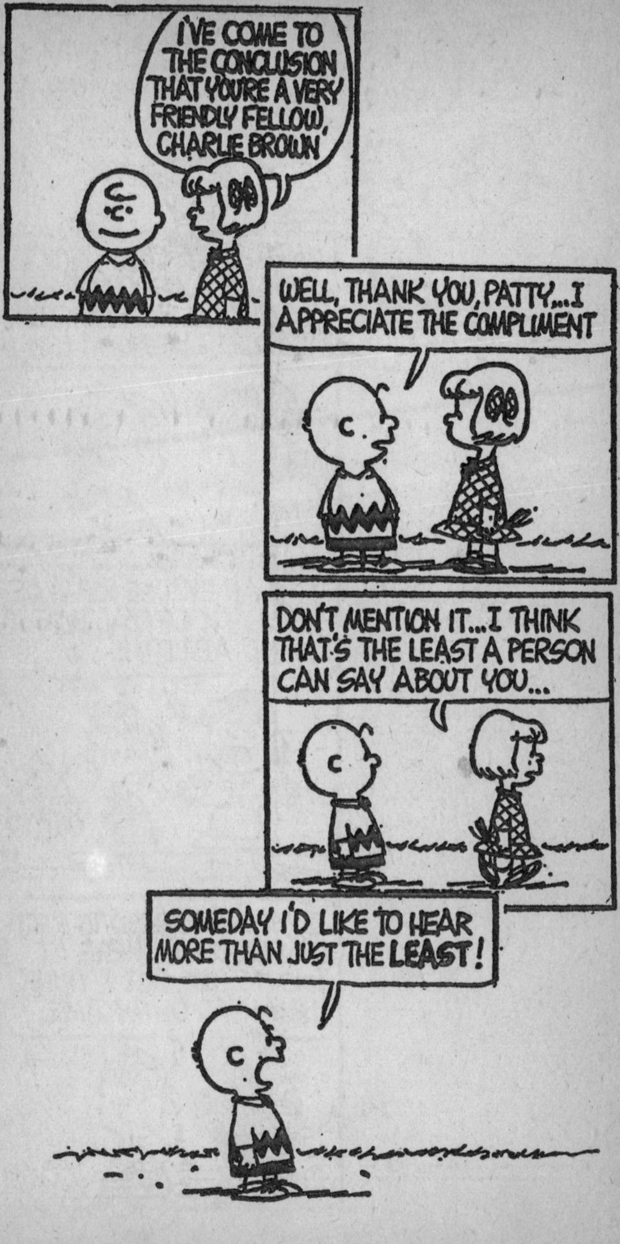
I'VE COME TO THE CONCLUSION THAT YOU'RE A VERY FRIENDLY FELLOW, CHARLIE BROWN
WELL, THANK YOU, PATTY...I APPRECIATE THE COMPLIMENT
DON'T MENTION IT...I THINK THAT'S THE LEAST A PERSON CAN SAY ABOUT YOU...
SOMEDAY I'D LIKE TO HEAR MORE THAN JUST THE **LEAST**!

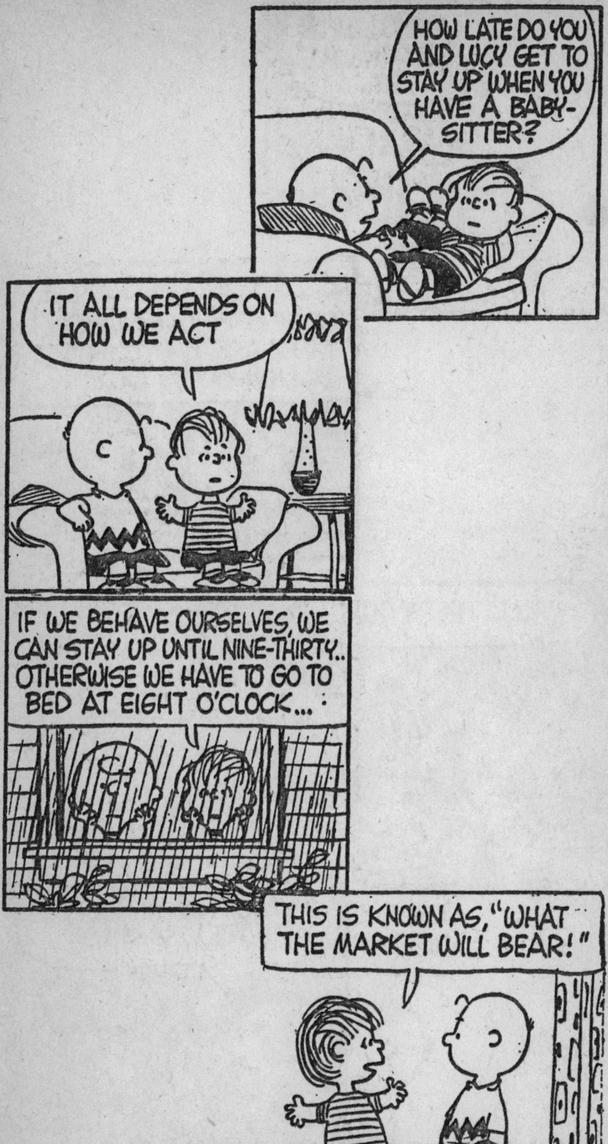
HOW LATE DO YOU AND LUCY GET TO STAY UP WHEN YOU HAVE A BABY-SITTER?
IT ALL DEPENDS ON HOW WE ACT
IF WE BEHAVE OURSELVES, WE CAN STAY UP UNTIL NINE-THIRTY.. OTHERWISE WE HAVE TO GO TO BED AT EIGHT O'CLOCK...
THIS IS KNOWN AS, "WHAT THE MARKET WILL BEAR!"

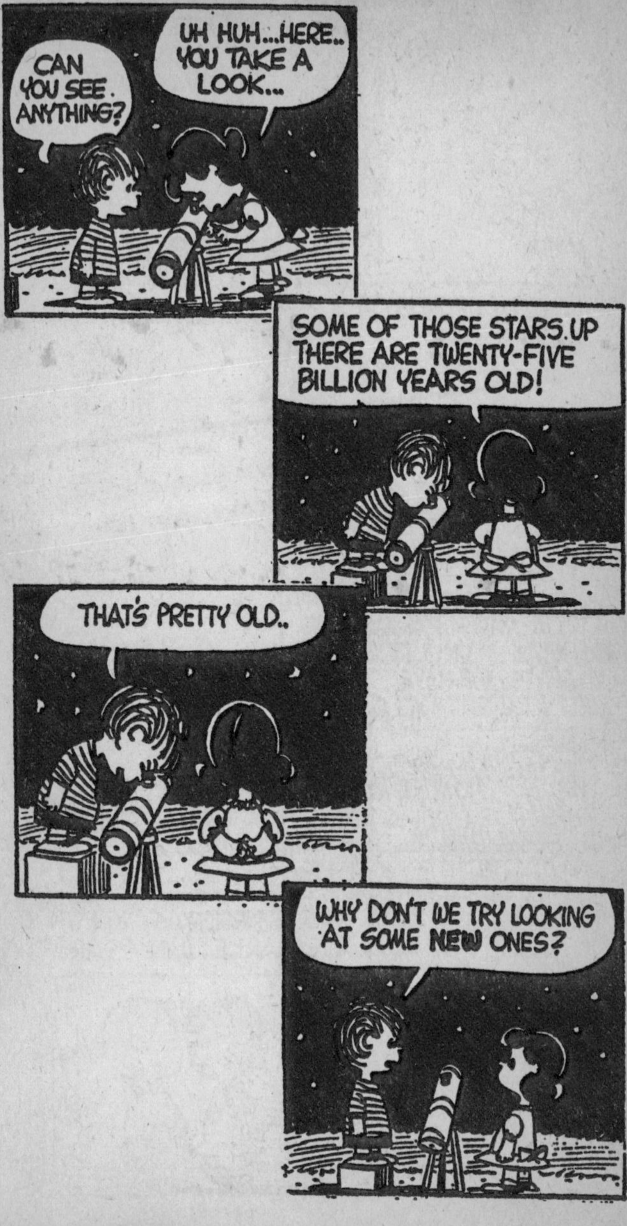
CAN YOU SEE ANYTHING?
UH HUH...HERE.. YOU TAKE A LOOK...
SOME OF THOSE STARS UP THERE ARE TWENTY-FIVE BILLION YEARS OLD!
THAT'S PRETTY OLD..
WHY DON'T WE TRY LOOKING AT SOME NEW ONES?

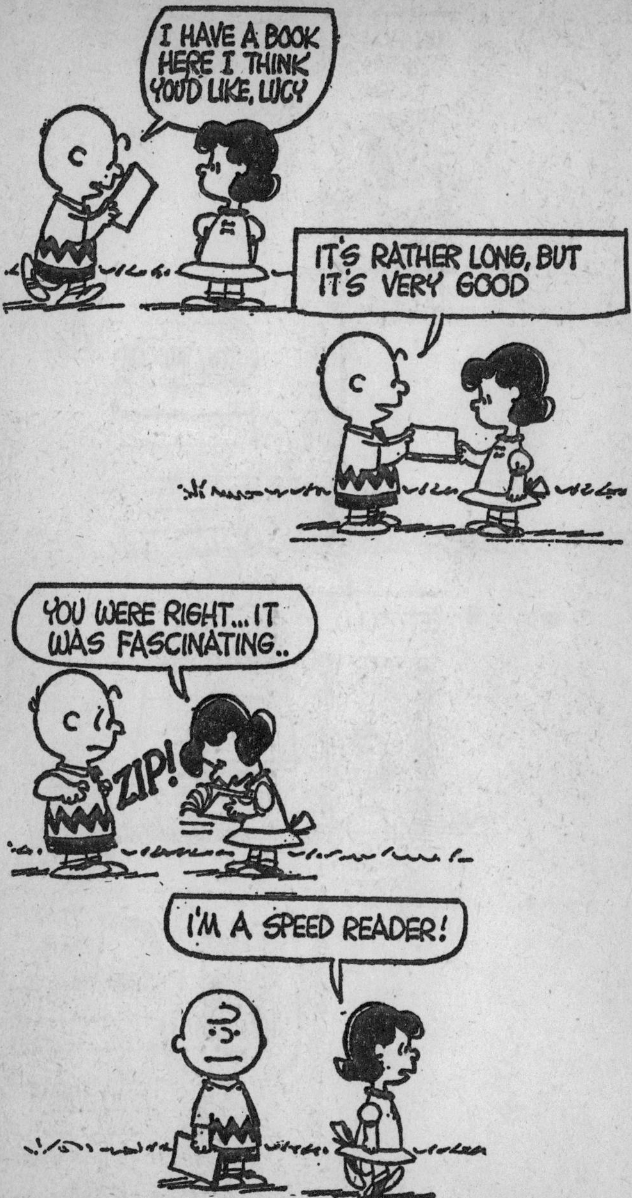

I HAVE A BOOK HERE I THINK YOU'D LIKE, LUCY
IT'S RATHER LONG, BUT IT'S VERY GOOD
YOU WERE RIGHT... IT WAS FASCINATING..
ZIP!
I'M A SPEED READER!

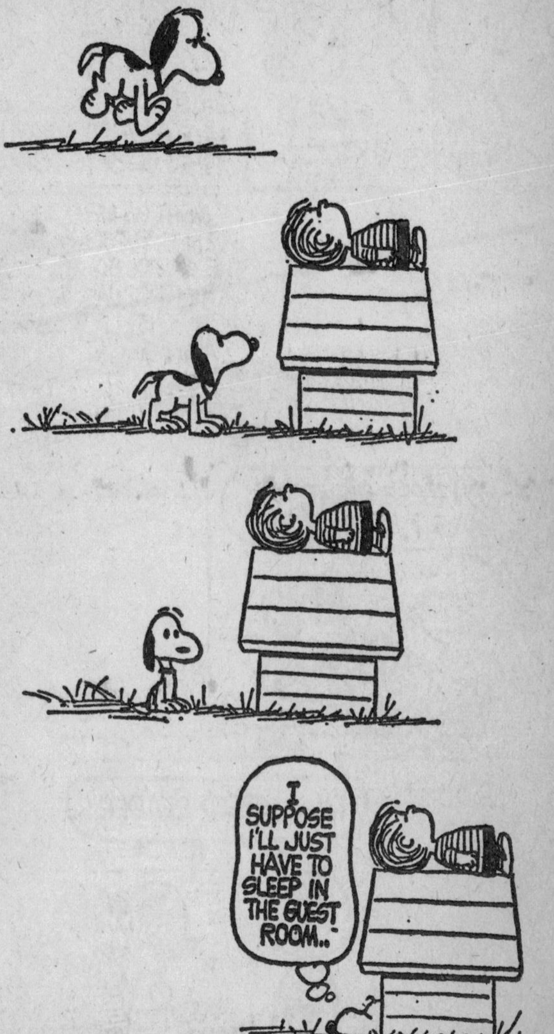
I SUPPOSE I'LL JUST HAVE TO SLEEP IN THE GUEST ROOM..

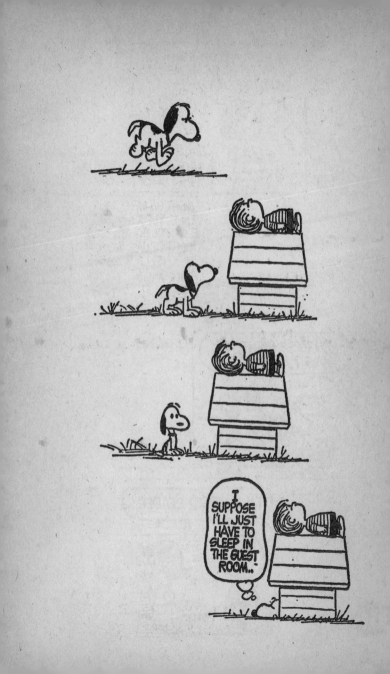

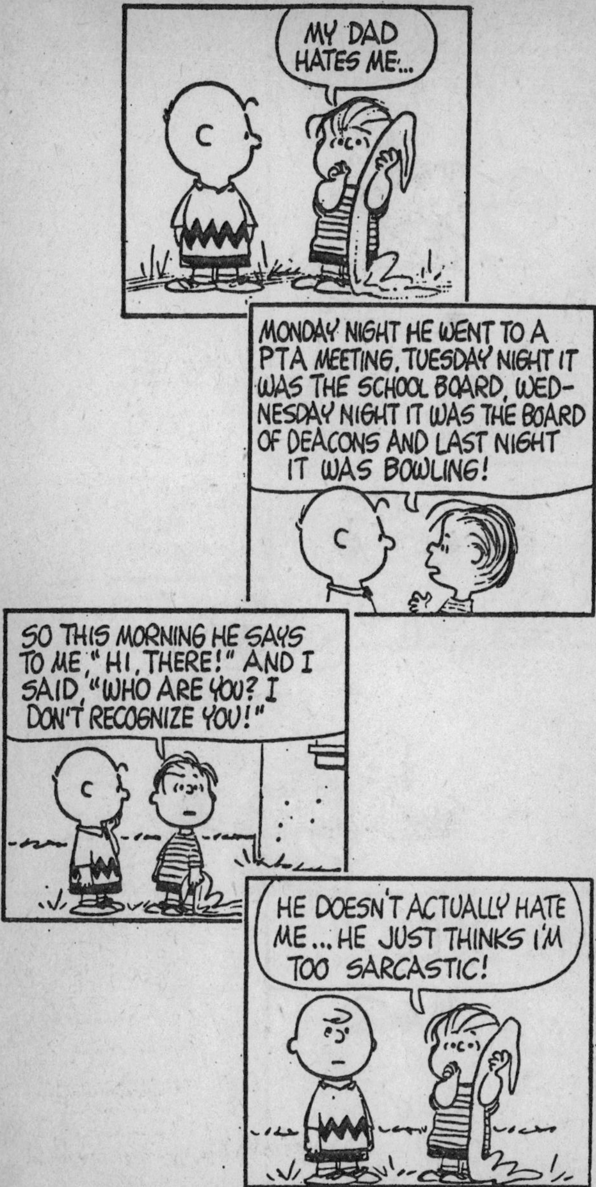
MY DAD HATES ME...
MONDAY NIGHT HE WENT TO A PTA MEETING, TUESDAY NIGHT IT WAS THE SCHOOL BOARD, WEDNESDAY NIGHT IT WAS THE BOARD OF DEACONS AND LAST NIGHT IT WAS BOWLING!
SO THIS MORNING HE SAYS TO ME, "HI, THERE!" AND I SAID, "WHO ARE YOU? I DON'T RECOGNIZE YOU!"
HE DOESN'T ACTUALLY HATE ME... HE JUST THINKS I'M TOO SARCASTIC!

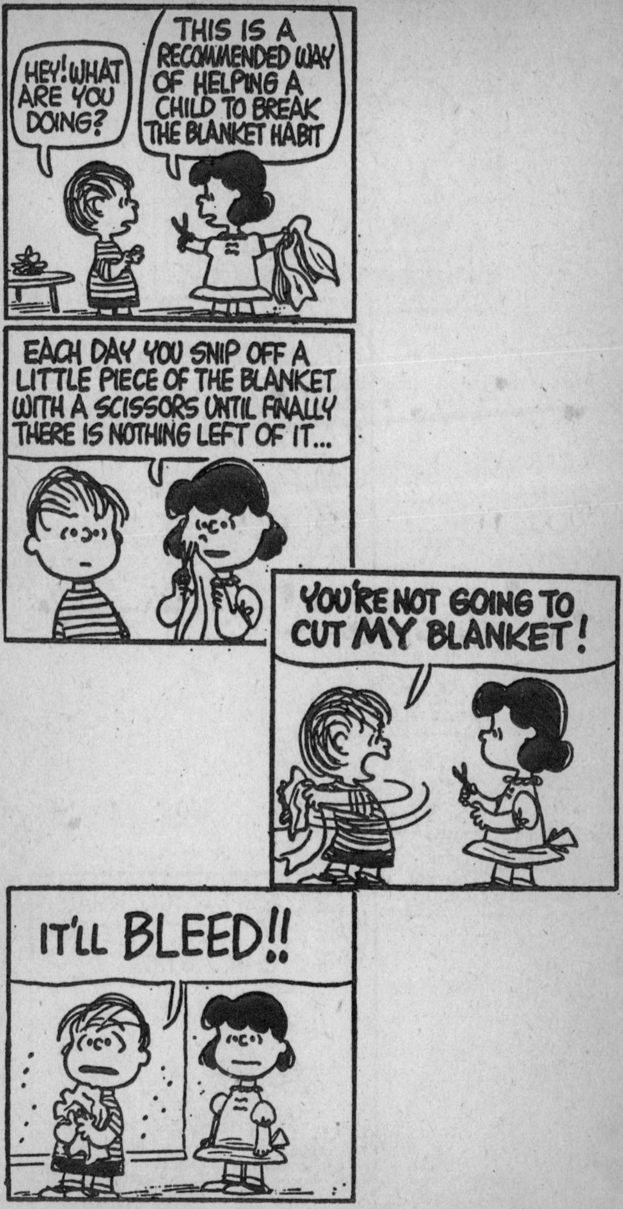
HEY! WHAT ARE YOU DOING?
THIS IS A RECOMMENDED WAY OF HELPING A CHILD TO BREAK THE BLANKET HABIT
EACH DAY YOU SNIP OFF A LITTLE PIECE OF THE BLANKET WITH A SCISSORS UNTIL FINALLY THERE IS NOTHING LEFT OF IT...
YOU'RE NOT GOING TO CUT MY BLANKET!
IT'LL BLEED!!

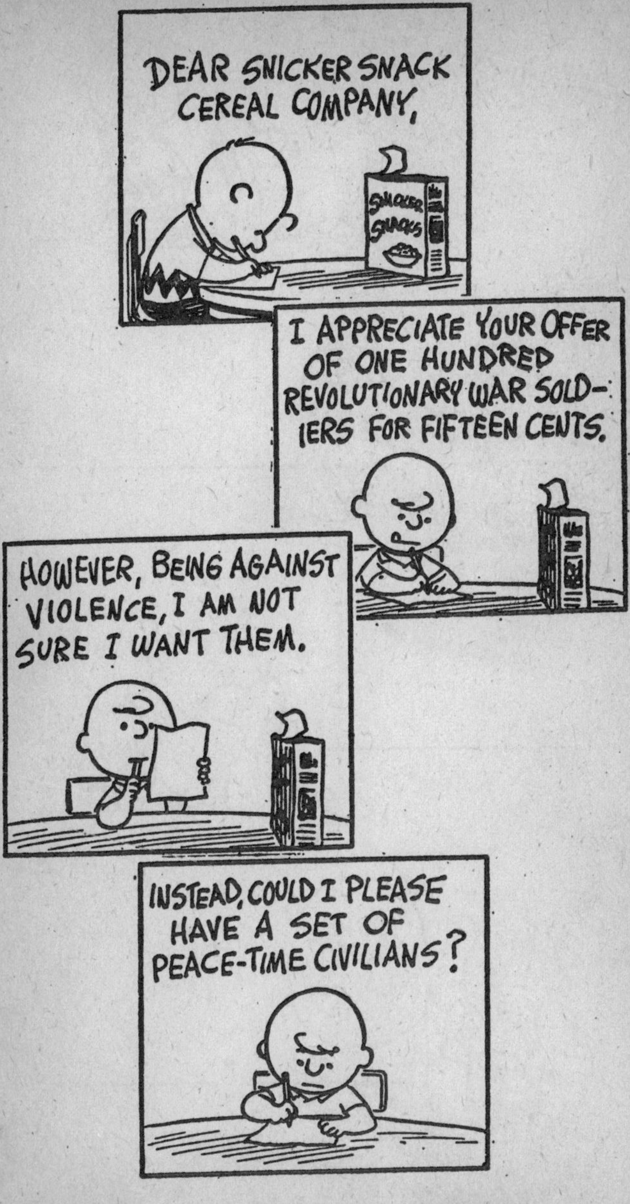
DEAR SNICKER SNACK CEREAL COMPANY,
SNICKER SNACKS
I APPRECIATE YOUR OFFER OF ONE HUNDRED REVOLUTIONARY WAR SOLD-IERS FOR FIFTEEN CENTS.
HOWEVER, BEING AGAINST VIOLENCE, I AM NOT SURE I WANT THEM.
INSTEAD, COULD I PLEASE HAVE A SET OF PEACE-TIME CIVILIANS?

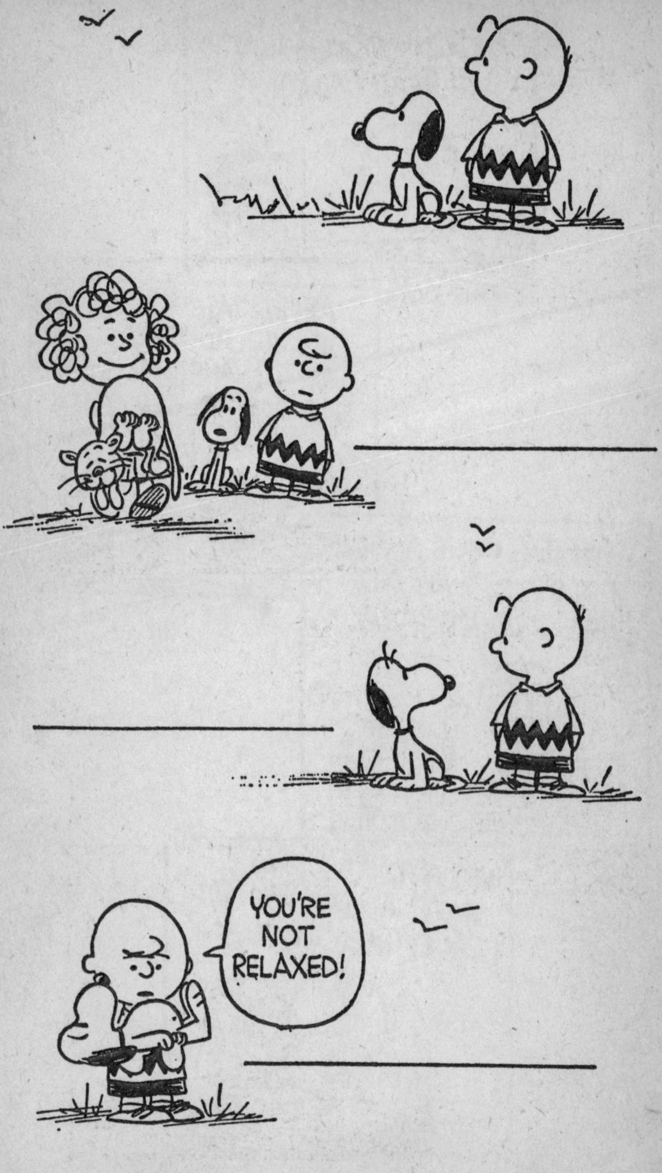
YOU'RE NOT RELAXED!

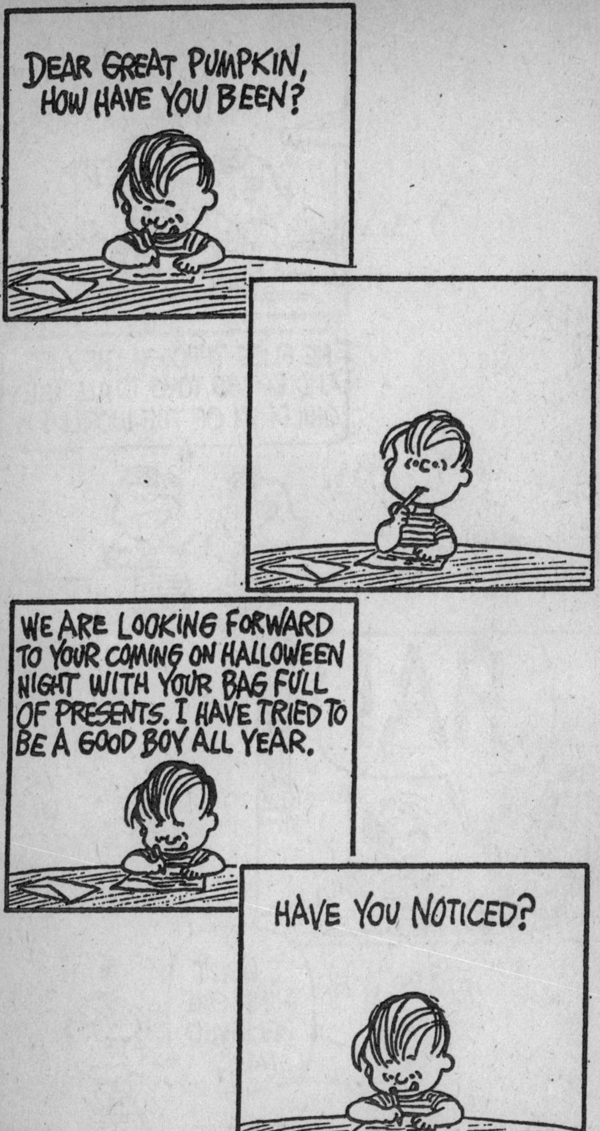
DEAR GREAT PUMPKIN, HOW HAVE YOU BEEN?
WE ARE LOOKING FORWARD TO YOUR COMING ON HALLOWEEN NIGHT WITH YOUR BAG FULL OF PRESENTS. I HAVE TRIED TO BE A GOOD BOY ALL YEAR.
HAVE YOU NOTICED?

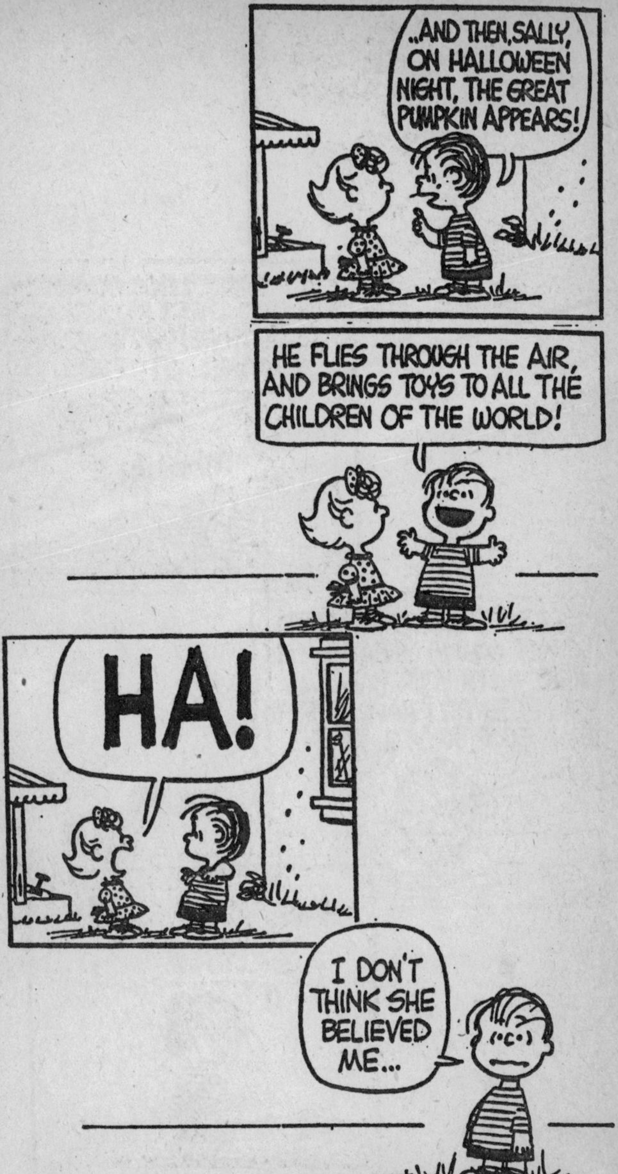
..AND THEN, SALLY, ON HALLOWEEN NIGHT, THE GREAT PUMPKIN APPEARS!
HE FLIES THROUGH THE AIR, AND BRINGS TOYS TO ALL THE CHILDREN OF THE WORLD!
HA!
I DON'T THINK SHE BELIEVED ME...

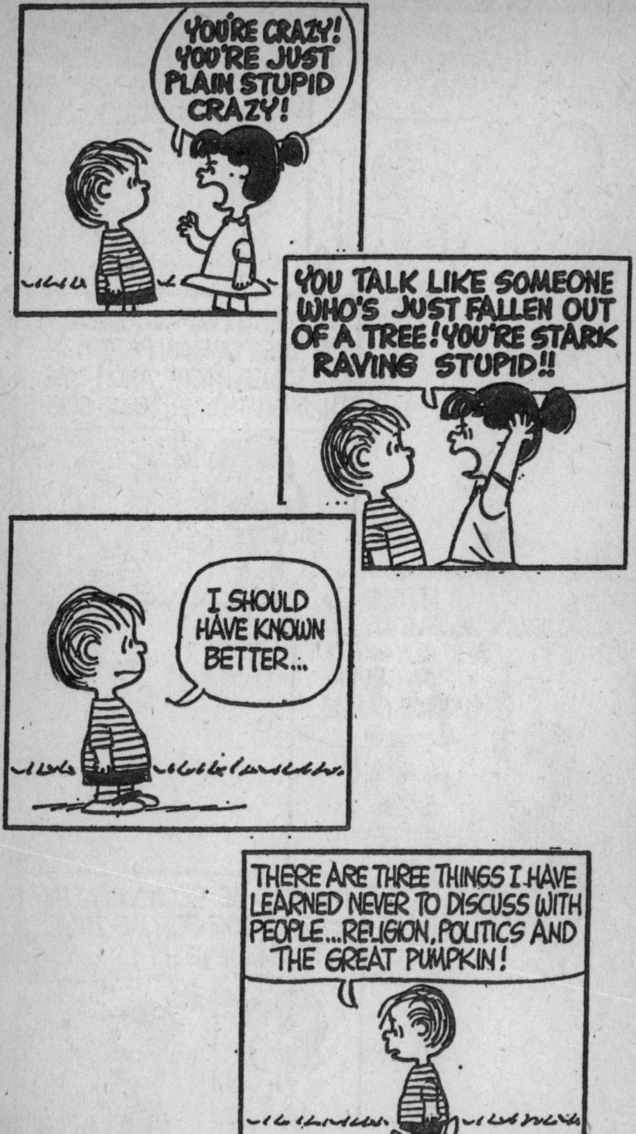
YOU'RE CRAZY! YOU'RE JUST PLAIN STUPID CRAZY!
YOU TALK LIKE SOMEONE WHO'S JUST FALLEN OUT OF A TREE! YOU'RE STARK RAVING STUPID!!
I SHOULD HAVE KNOWN BETTER...
THERE ARE THREE THINGS I HAVE LEARNED NEVER TO DISCUSS WITH PEOPLE...RELIGION, POLITICS AND THE GREAT PUMPKIN!

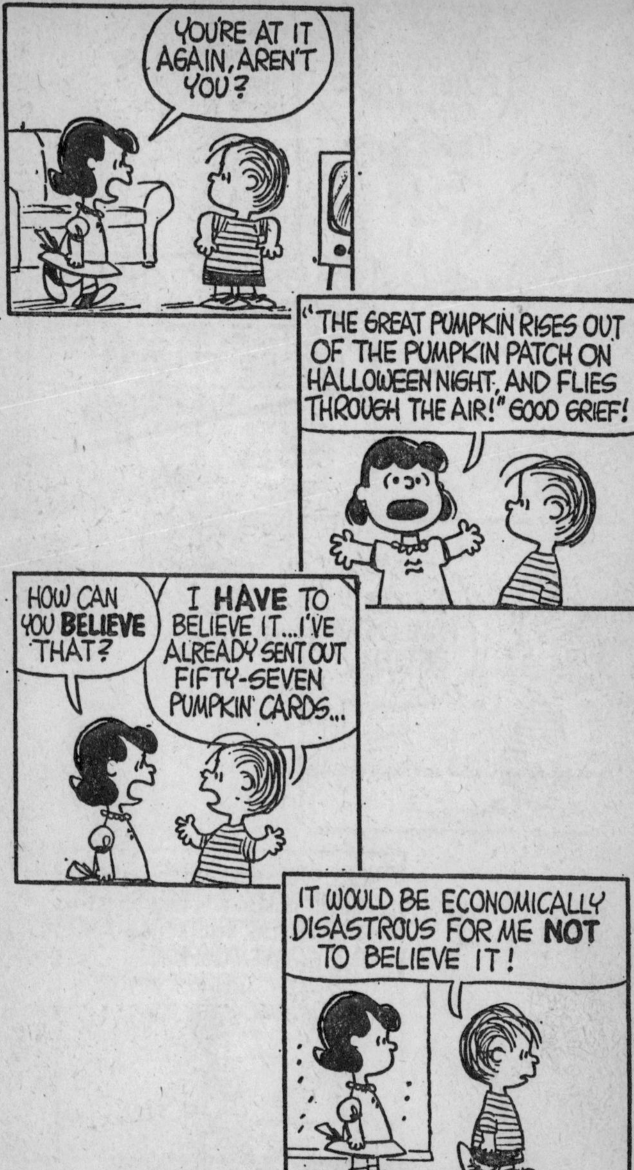
YOU'RE AT IT AGAIN, AREN'T YOU?
"THE GREAT PUMPKIN RISES OUT OF THE PUMPKIN PATCH ON HALLOWEEN NIGHT, AND FLIES THROUGH THE AIR!" GOOD GRIEF!
HOW CAN YOU **BELIEVE** THAT?
I **HAVE** TO BELIEVE IT...I'VE ALREADY SENT OUT FIFTY-SEVEN PUMPKIN CARDS...
IT WOULD BE ECONOMICALLY DISASTROUS FOR ME **NOT** TO BELIEVE IT!

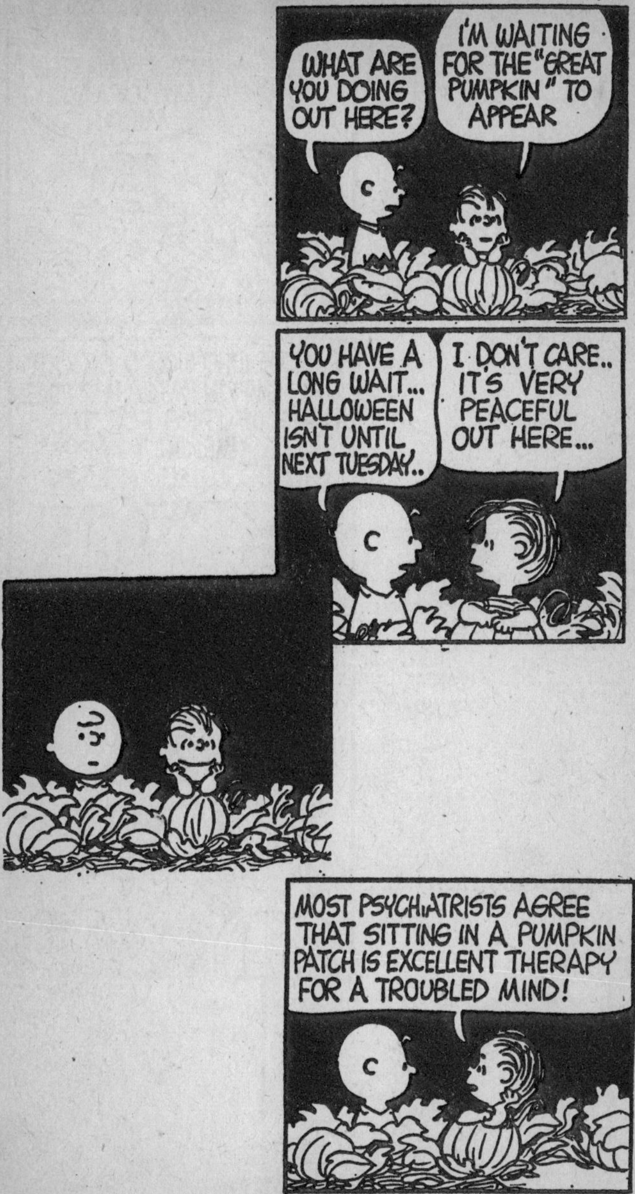
WHAT ARE YOU DOING OUT HERE?
I'M WAITING FOR THE "GREAT PUMPKIN" TO APPEAR
YOU HAVE A LONG WAIT... HALLOWEEN ISN'T UNTIL NEXT TUESDAY..
I DON'T CARE.. IT'S VERY PEACEFUL OUT HERE...
MOST PSYCHIATRISTS AGREE THAT SITTING IN A PUMPKIN PATCH IS EXCELLENT THERAPY FOR A TROUBLED MIND!

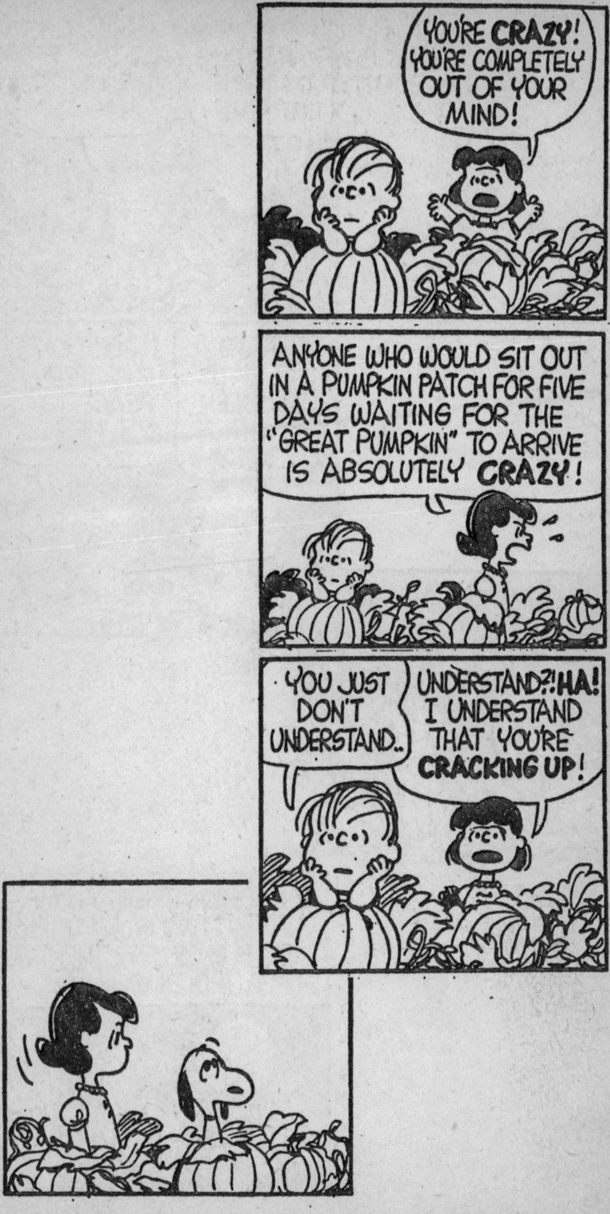
YOU'RE CRAZY! YOU'RE COMPLETELY OUT OF YOUR MIND!
ANYONE WHO WOULD SIT OUT IN A PUMPKIN PATCH FOR FIVE DAYS WAITING FOR THE "GREAT PUMPKIN" TO ARRIVE IS ABSOLUTELY CRAZY!
YOU JUST DON'T UNDERSTAND..
UNDERSTAND?! HA! I UNDERSTAND THAT YOU'RE CRACKING UP!

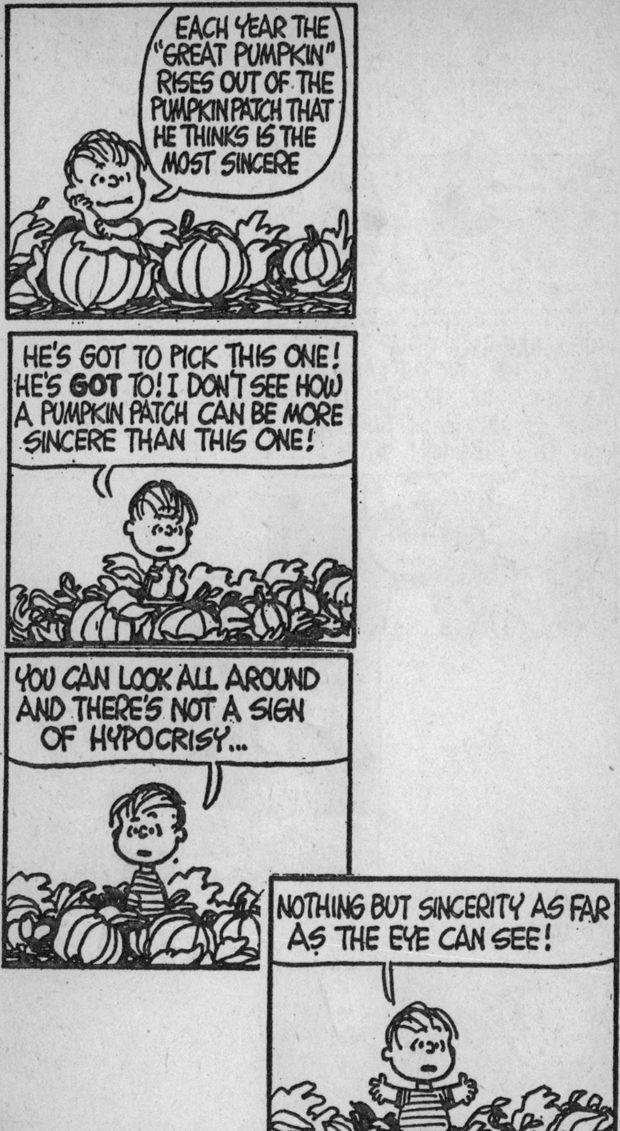
EACH YEAR THE "GREAT PUMPKIN" RISES OUT OF THE PUMPKIN PATCH THAT HE THINKS IS THE MOST SINCERE
HE'S GOT TO PICK THIS ONE! HE'S **GOT** TO! I DON'T SEE HOW A PUMPKIN PATCH CAN BE MORE SINCERE THAN THIS ONE!
YOU CAN LOOK ALL AROUND AND THERE'S NOT A SIGN OF HYPOCRISY...
NOTHING BUT SINCERITY AS FAR AS THE EYE CAN SEE!

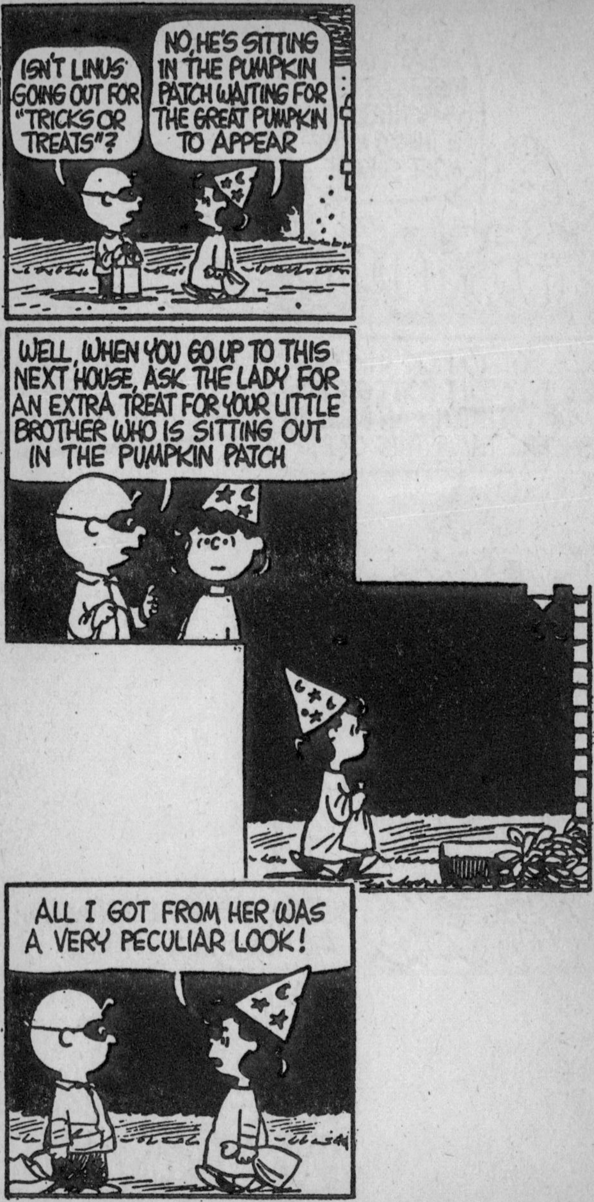
ISN'T LINUS GOING OUT FOR "TRICKS OR TREATS"?
NO, HE'S SITTING IN THE PUMPKIN PATCH WAITING FOR THE GREAT PUMPKIN TO APPEAR
WELL, WHEN YOU GO UP TO THIS NEXT HOUSE, ASK THE LADY FOR AN EXTRA TREAT FOR YOUR LITTLE BROTHER WHO IS SITTING OUT IN THE PUMPKIN PATCH
ALL I GOT FROM HER WAS A VERY PECULIAR LOOK!

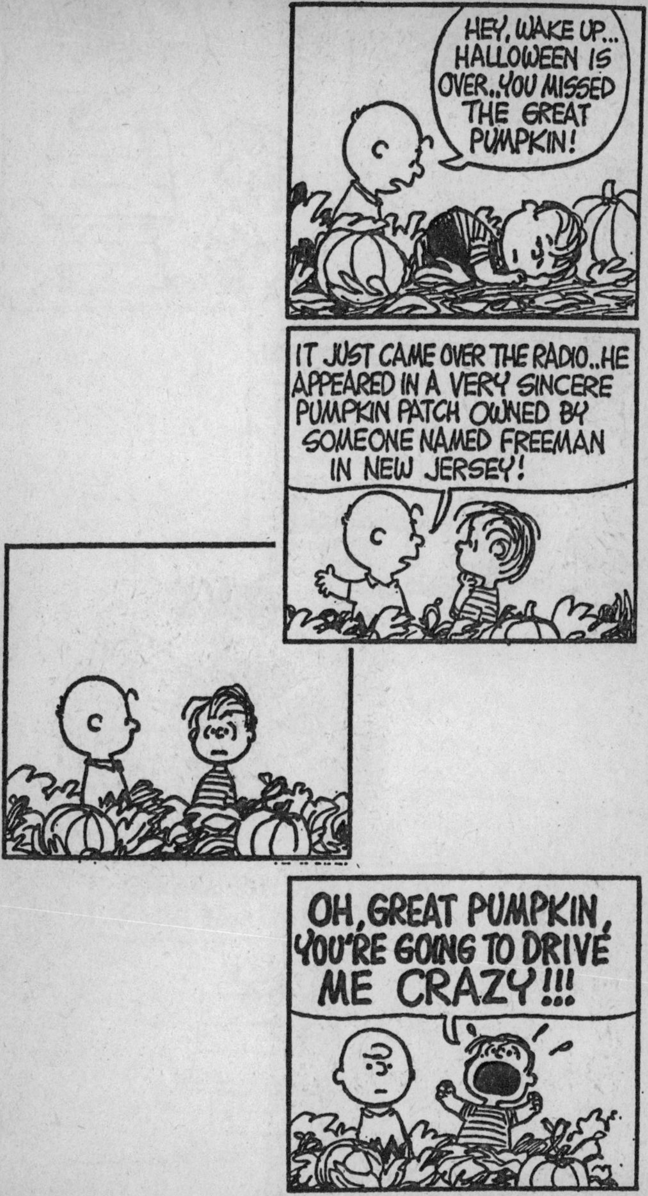
HEY, WAKE UP... HALLOWEEN IS OVER..YOU MISSED THE GREAT PUMPKIN!
IT JUST CAME OVER THE RADIO..HE APPEARED IN A VERY SINCERE PUMPKIN PATCH OWNED BY SOMEONE NAMED FREEMAN IN NEW JERSEY!
OH, GREAT PUMPKIN, YOU'RE GOING TO DRIVE ME CRAZY!!!

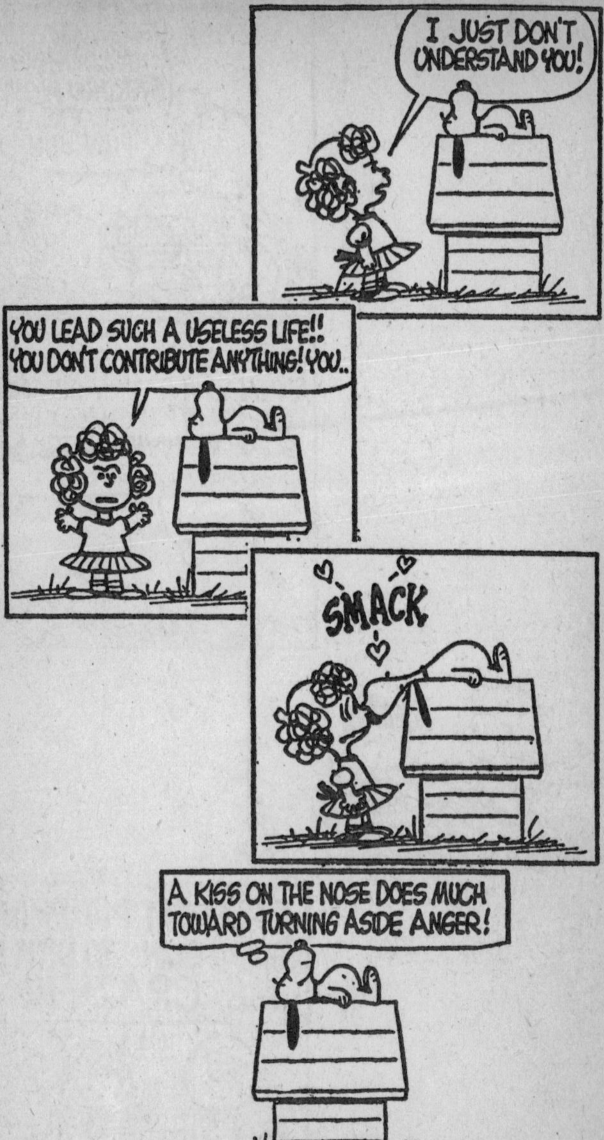
I JUST DON'T UNDERSTAND YOU!
YOU LEAD SUCH A USELESS LIFE!! YOU DON'T CONTRIBUTE ANYTHING! YOU..
SMACK
A KISS ON THE NOSE DOES MUCH TOWARD TURNING ASIDE ANGER!

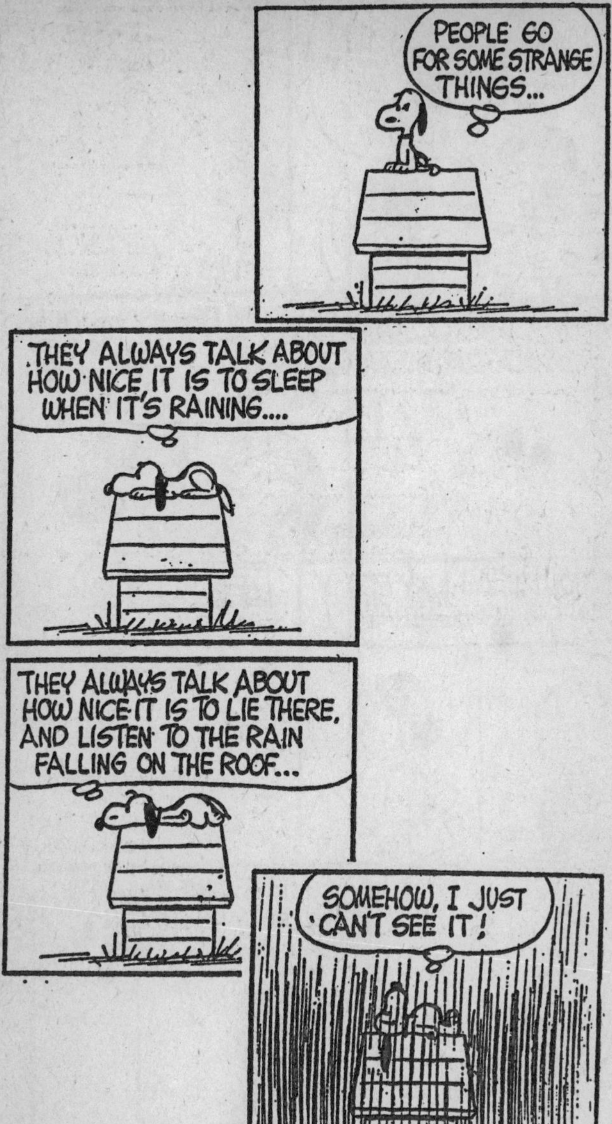
PEOPLE GO FOR SOME STRANGE THINGS...
THEY ALWAYS TALK ABOUT HOW NICE IT IS TO SLEEP WHEN IT'S RAINING....
THEY ALWAYS TALK ABOUT HOW NICE IT IS TO LIE THERE, AND LISTEN TO THE RAIN FALLING ON THE ROOF...
SOMEHOW, I JUST CAN'T SEE IT!

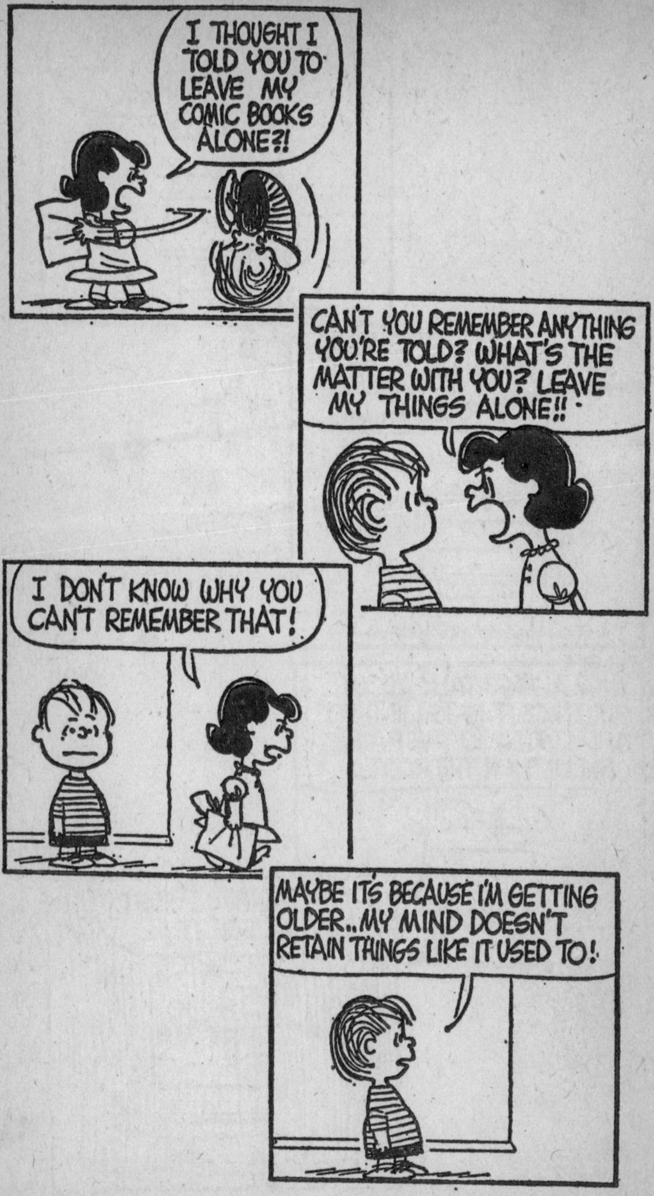
I THOUGHT I TOLD YOU TO LEAVE MY COMIC BOOKS ALONE?!
CAN'T YOU REMEMBER ANYTHING YOU'RE TOLD? WHAT'S THE MATTER WITH YOU? LEAVE MY THINGS ALONE!!
I DON'T KNOW WHY YOU CAN'T REMEMBER THAT!
MAYBE IT'S BECAUSE I'M GETTING OLDER..MY MIND DOESN'T RETAIN THINGS LIKE IT USED TO!

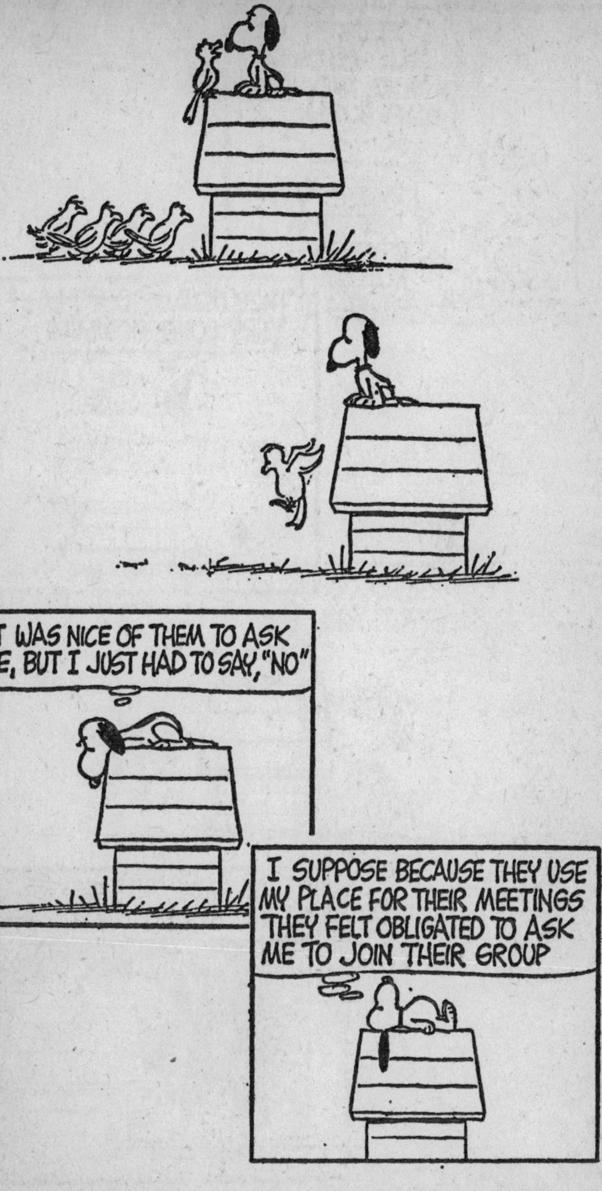

IT WAS NICE OF THEM TO ASK ME, BUT I JUST HAD TO SAY, "NO"
I SUPPOSE BECAUSE THEY USE MY PLACE FOR THEIR MEETINGS THEY FELT OBLIGATED TO ASK ME TO JOIN THEIR GROUP

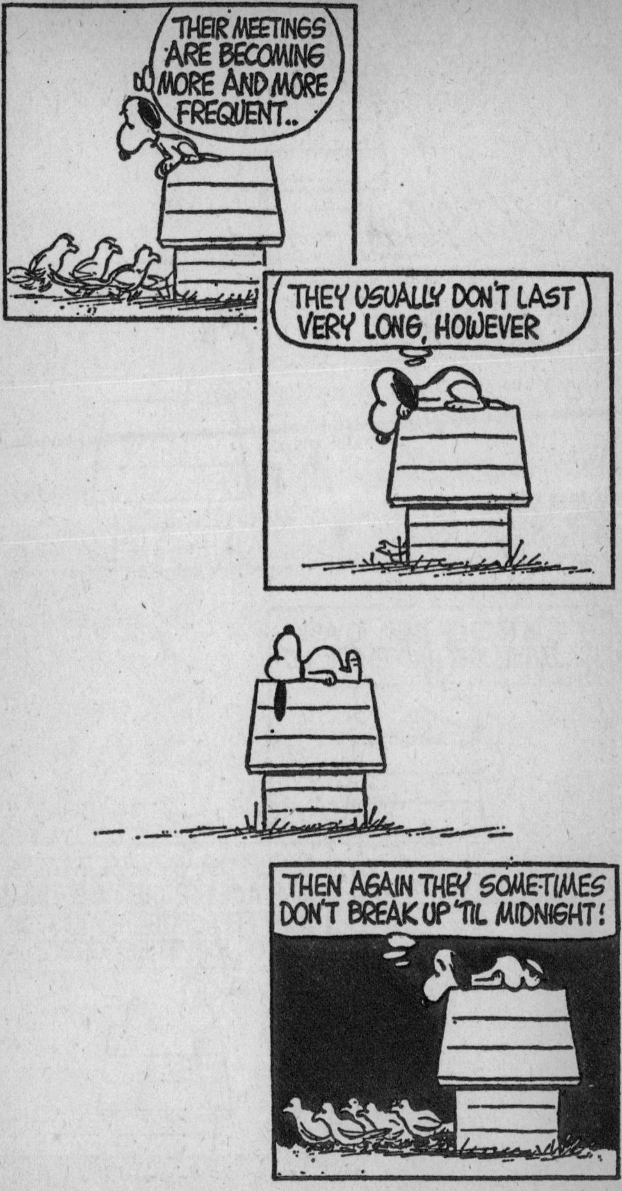
THEIR MEETINGS ARE BECOMING MORE AND MORE FREQUENT..
THEY USUALLY DON'T LAST VERY LONG, HOWEVER
THEN AGAIN THEY SOMETIMES DON'T BREAK UP 'TIL MIDNIGHT!

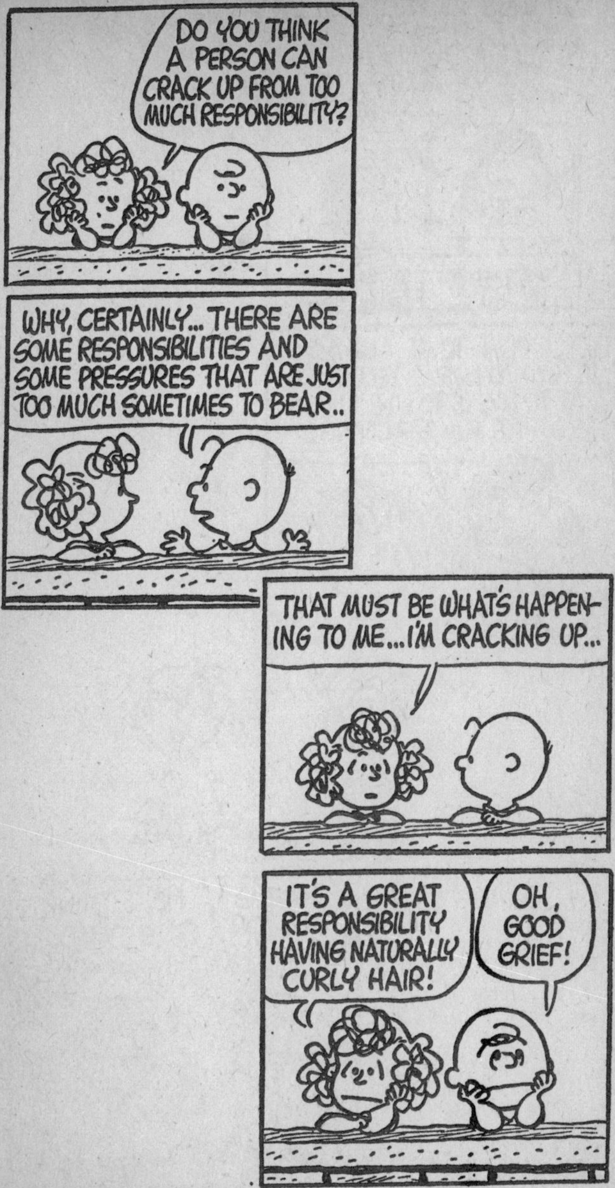
DO YOU THINK A PERSON CAN CRACK UP FROM TOO MUCH RESPONSIBILITY?
WHY, CERTAINLY... THERE ARE SOME RESPONSIBILITIES AND SOME PRESSURES THAT ARE JUST TOO MUCH SOMETIMES TO BEAR..
THAT MUST BE WHAT'S HAPPENING TO ME... I'M CRACKING UP...
IT'S A GREAT RESPONSIBILITY HAVING NATURALLY CURLY HAIR!
OH, GOOD GRIEF!

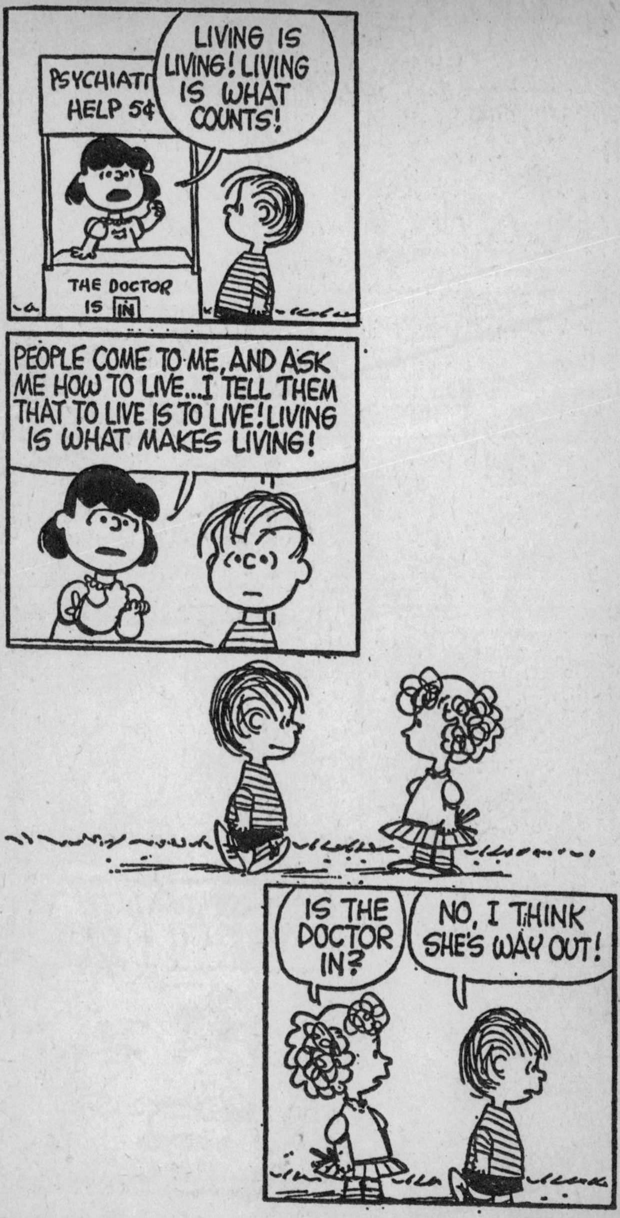
PSYCHIATRIC HELP 5¢
LIVING IS LIVING! LIVING IS WHAT COUNTS!
THE DOCTOR IS IN
PEOPLE COME TO ME, AND ASK ME HOW TO LIVE...I TELL THEM THAT TO LIVE IS TO LIVE! LIVING IS WHAT MAKES LIVING!
IS THE DOCTOR IN?
NO, I THINK SHE'S WAY OUT!

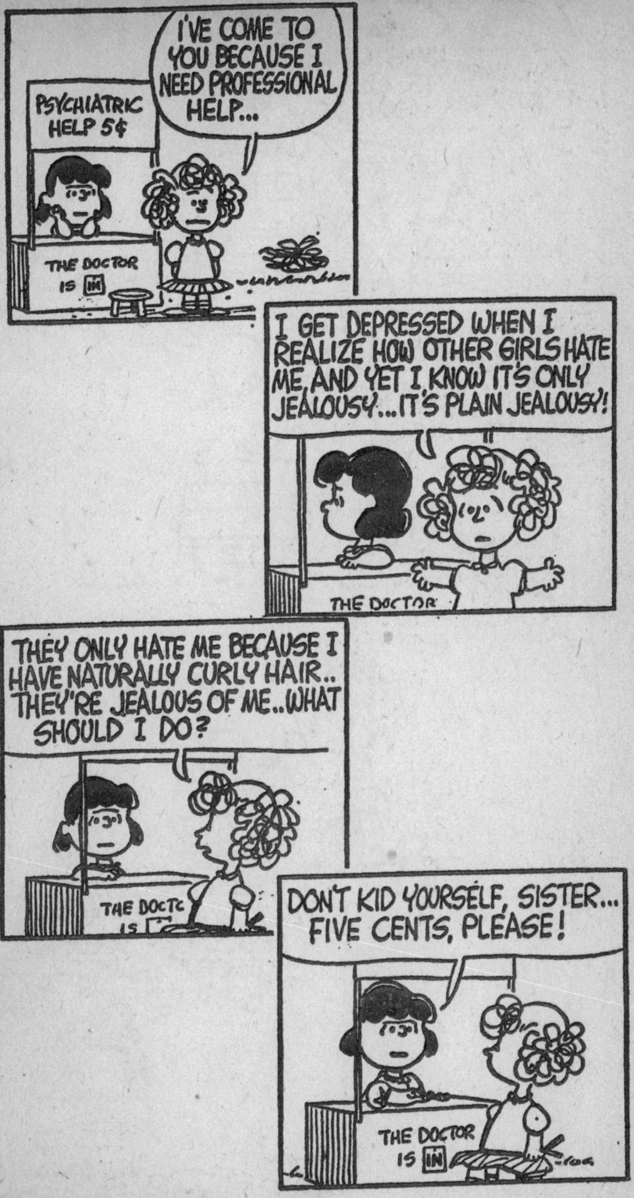
I'VE COME TO YOU BECAUSE I NEED PROFESSIONAL HELP...
PSYCHIATRIC HELP 5¢
THE DOCTOR IS IN
I GET DEPRESSED WHEN I REALIZE HOW OTHER GIRLS HATE ME, AND YET I KNOW IT'S ONLY JEALOUSY...IT'S PLAIN JEALOUSY!
THE DOCTOR
THEY ONLY HATE ME BECAUSE I HAVE NATURALLY CURLY HAIR.. THEY'RE JEALOUS OF ME..WHAT SHOULD I DO?
DON'T KID YOURSELF, SISTER... FIVE CENTS, PLEASE!
THE DOCTOR IS IN

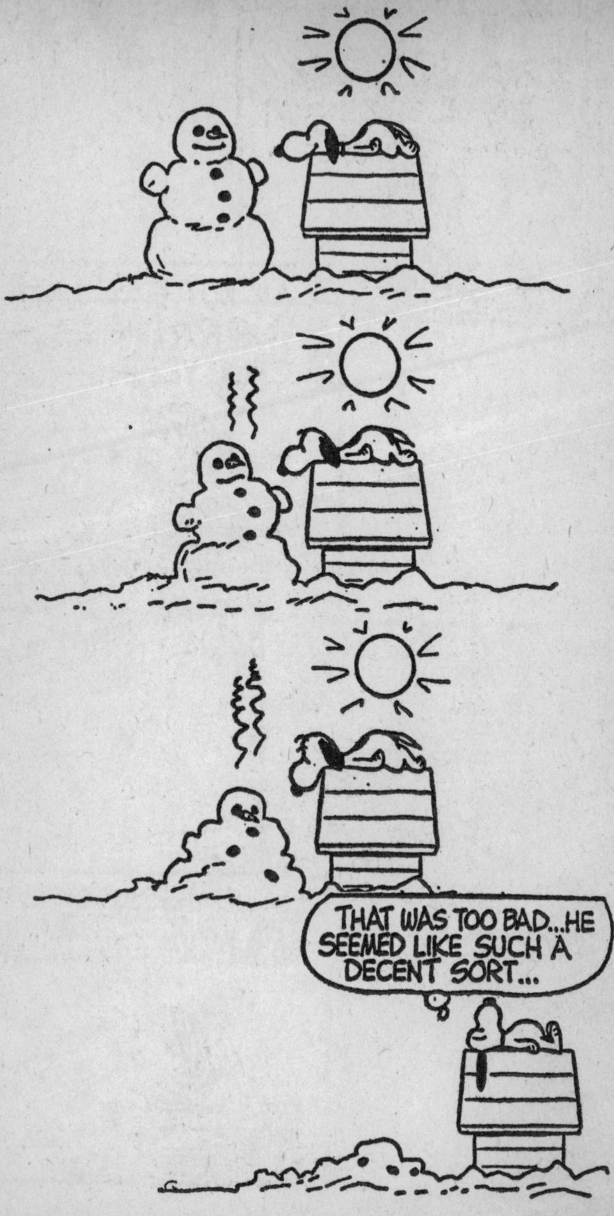
THAT WAS TOO BAD...HE SEEMED LIKE SUCH A DECENT SORT...

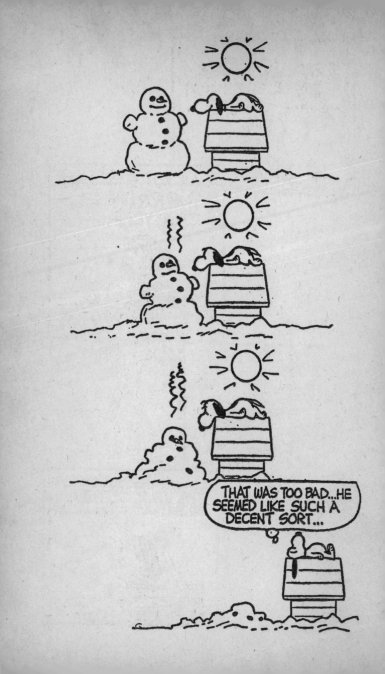

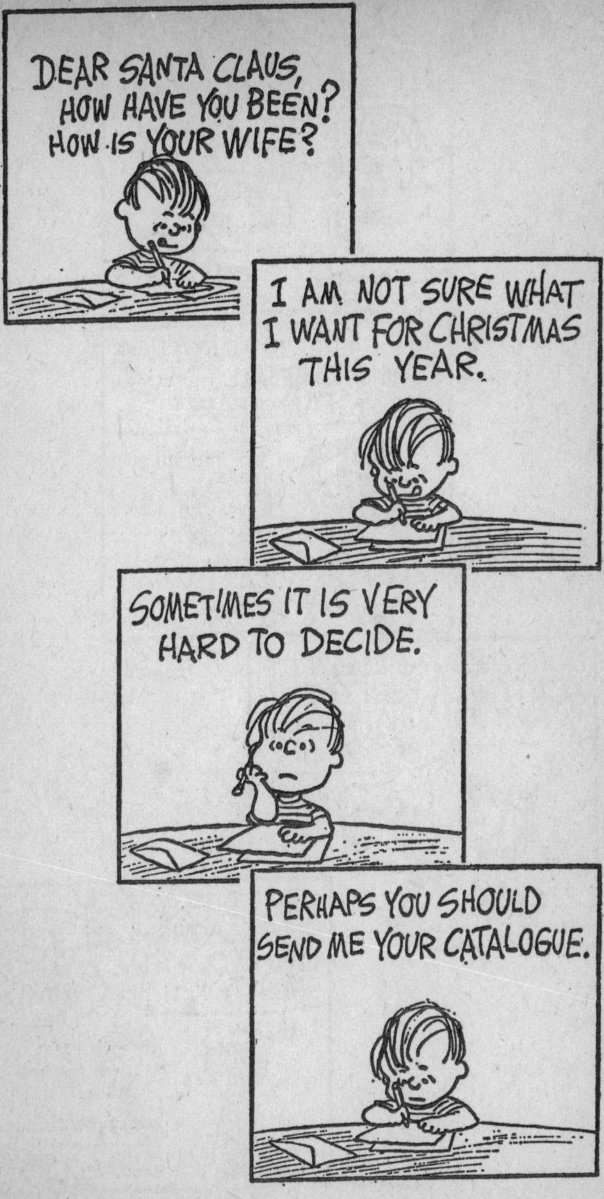
DEAR SANTA CLAUS,
HOW HAVE YOU BEEN?
HOW IS YOUR WIFE?
I AM NOT SURE WHAT I WANT FOR CHRISTMAS THIS YEAR.
SOMETIMES IT IS VERY HARD TO DECIDE.
PERHAPS YOU SHOULD SEND ME YOUR CATALOGUE.

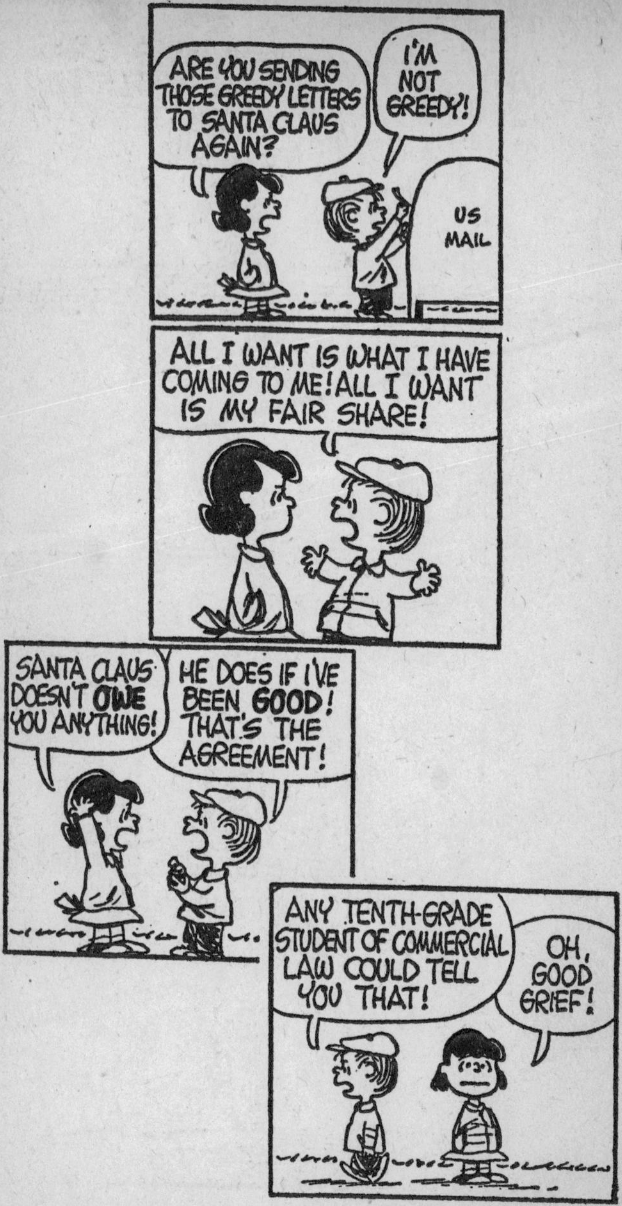
ARE YOU SENDING THOSE GREEDY LETTERS TO SANTA CLAUS AGAIN?
I'M NOT GREEDY!
US MAIL
ALL I WANT IS WHAT I HAVE COMING TO ME! ALL I WANT IS MY FAIR SHARE!
SANTA CLAUS DOESN'T OWE YOU ANYTHING!
HE DOES IF I'VE BEEN GOOD! THAT'S THE AGREEMENT!
ANY TENTH-GRADE STUDENT OF COMMERCIAL LAW COULD TELL YOU THAT!
OH, GOOD GRIEF!

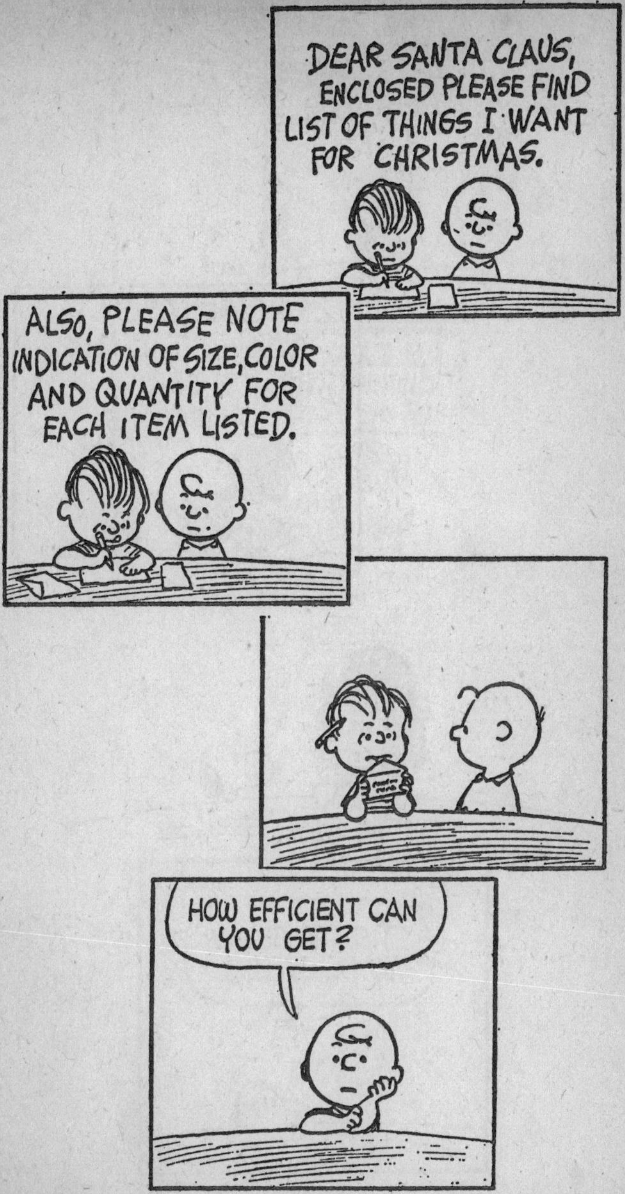
DEAR SANTA CLAUS,
ENCLOSED PLEASE FIND LIST OF THINGS I WANT FOR CHRISTMAS.
ALSO, PLEASE NOTE INDICATION OF SIZE, COLOR AND QUANTITY FOR EACH ITEM LISTED.
HOW EFFICIENT CAN YOU GET?

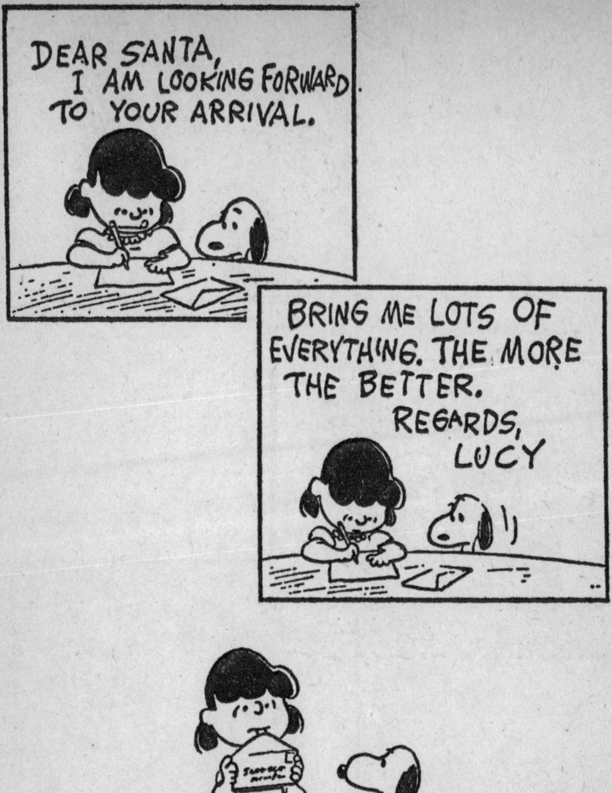
DEAR SANTA,
I AM LOOKING FORWARD TO YOUR ARRIVAL.
BRING ME LOTS OF EVERYTHING. THE MORE THE BETTER.
REGARDS,
LUCY
'TIS THE SEASON TO BE GREEDY

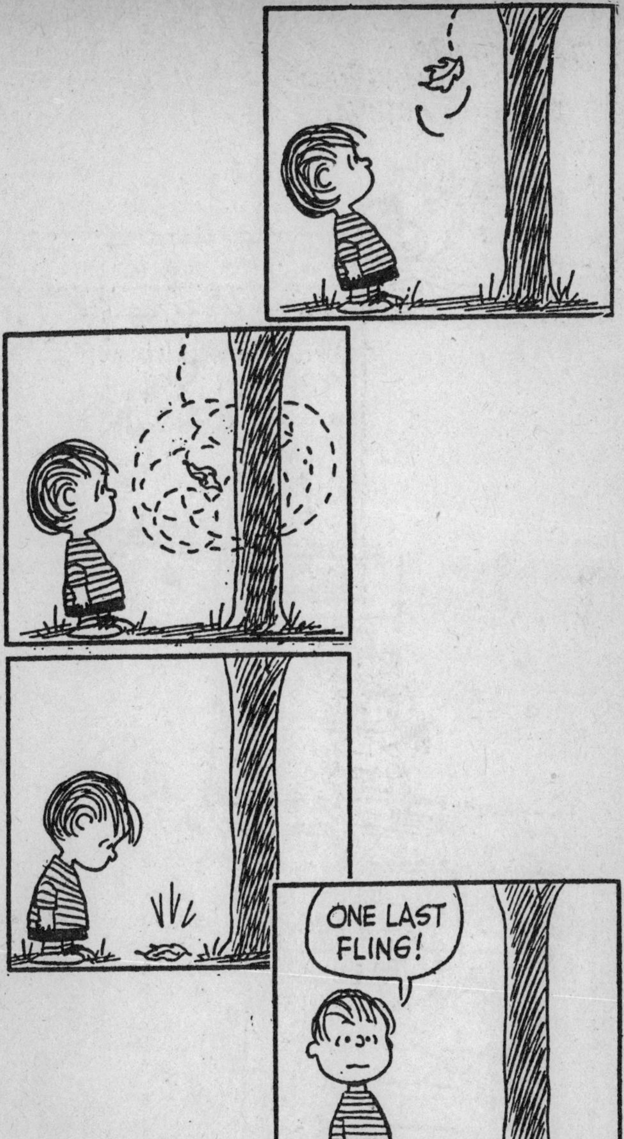
ONE LAST FLING!

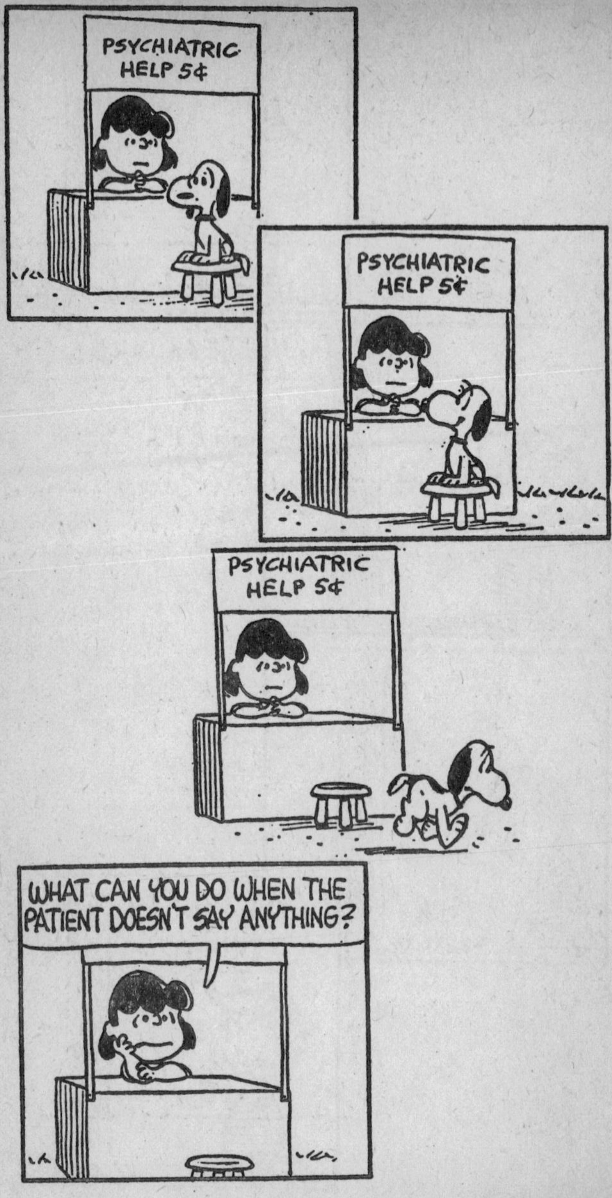

PSYCHIATRIC HELP 5¢
PSYCHIATRIC HELP 5¢
PSYCHIATRIC HELP 5¢
WHAT CAN YOU DO WHEN THE PATIENT DOESN'T SAY ANYTHING?

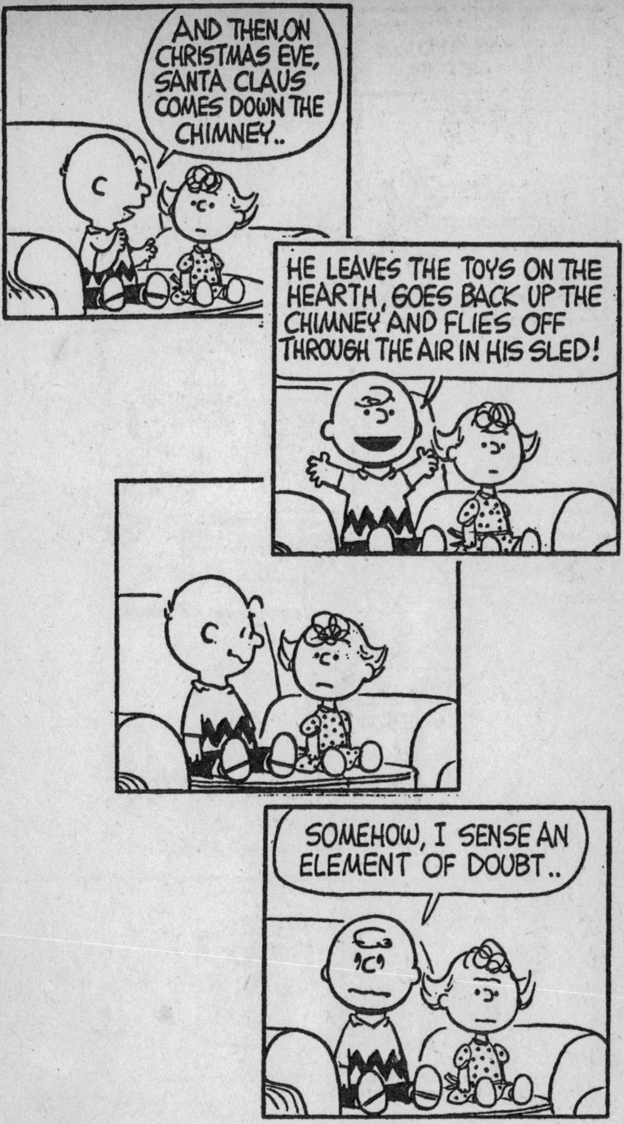
AND THEN, ON CHRISTMAS EVE, SANTA CLAUS COMES DOWN THE CHIMNEY..
HE LEAVES THE TOYS ON THE HEARTH, GOES BACK UP THE CHIMNEY AND FLIES OFF THROUGH THE AIR IN HIS SLED!
SOMEHOW, I SENSE AN ELEMENT OF DOUBT..

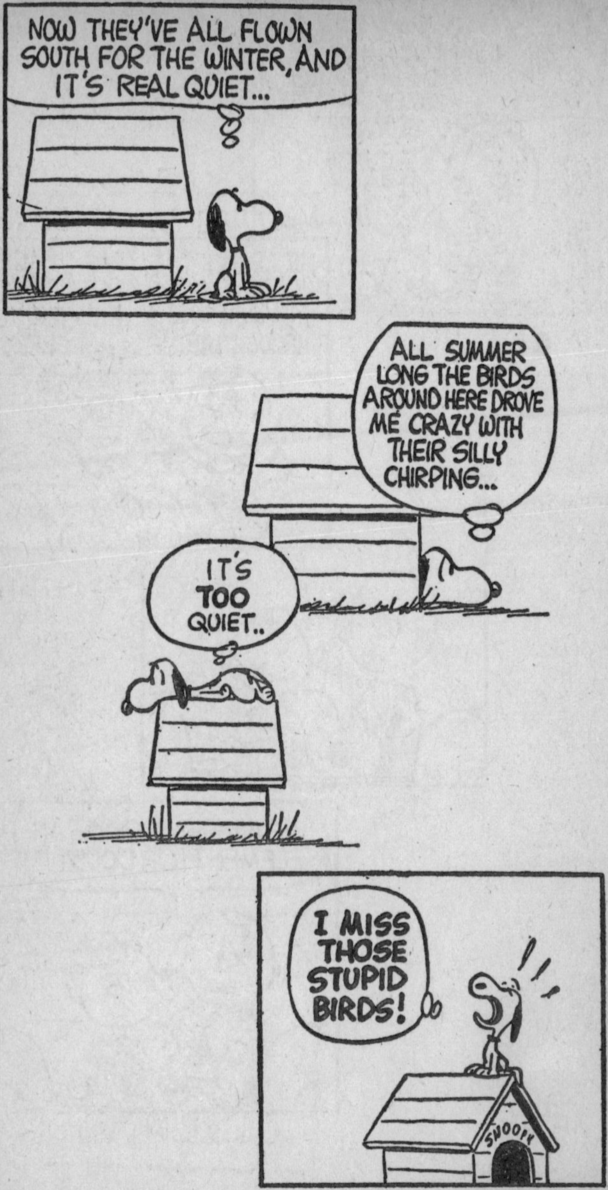
NOW THEY'VE ALL FLOWN SOUTH FOR THE WINTER, AND IT'S REAL QUIET...
ALL SUMMER LONG THE BIRDS AROUND HERE DROVE ME CRAZY WITH THEIR SILLY CHIRPING...
IT'S TOO QUIET..
I MISS THOSE STUPID BIRDS!
SNOOPY

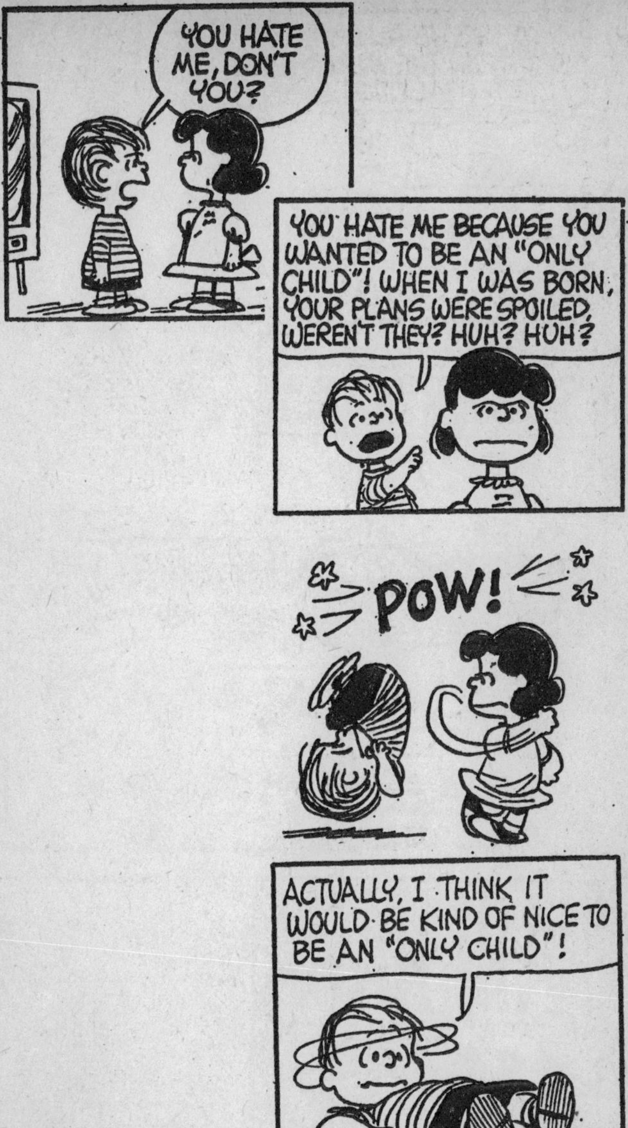
YOU HATE ME, DON'T YOU?
YOU HATE ME BECAUSE YOU WANTED TO BE AN "ONLY CHILD"! WHEN I WAS BORN, YOUR PLANS WERE SPOILED, WEREN'T THEY? HUH? HUH?
POW!
ACTUALLY, I THINK IT WOULD BE KIND OF NICE TO BE AN "ONLY CHILD"!

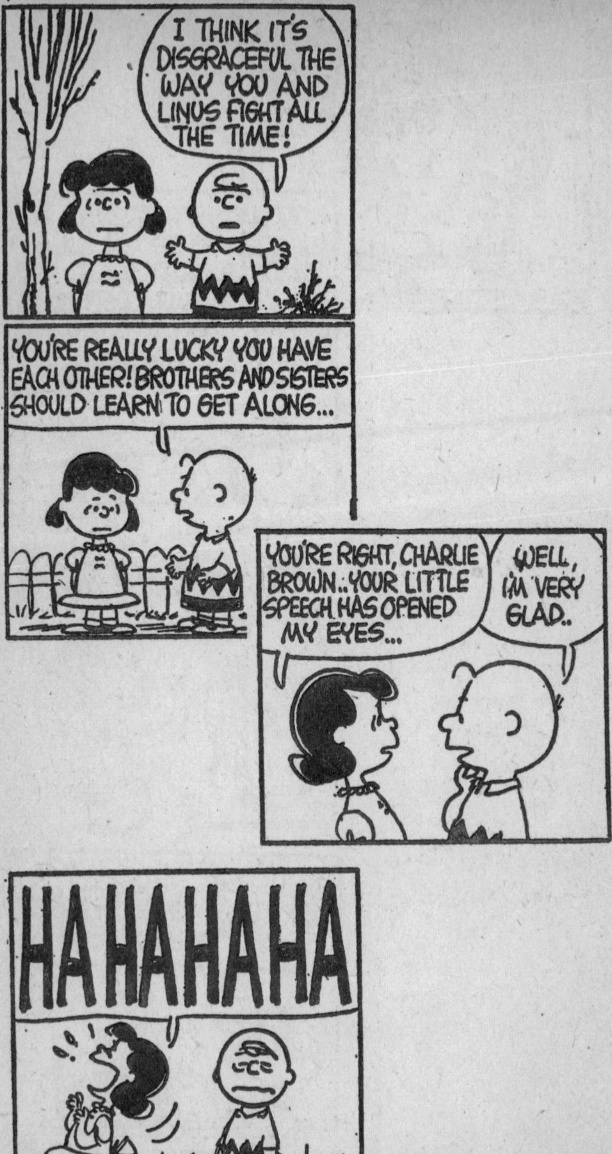
I THINK IT'S DISGRACEFUL THE WAY YOU AND LINUS FIGHT ALL THE TIME!
YOU'RE REALLY LUCKY YOU HAVE EACH OTHER! BROTHERS AND SISTERS SHOULD LEARN TO GET ALONG...
YOU'RE RIGHT, CHARLIE BROWN.. YOUR LITTLE SPEECH HAS OPENED MY EYES...
WELL, I'M VERY GLAD..
HA HA HA HA HA HA

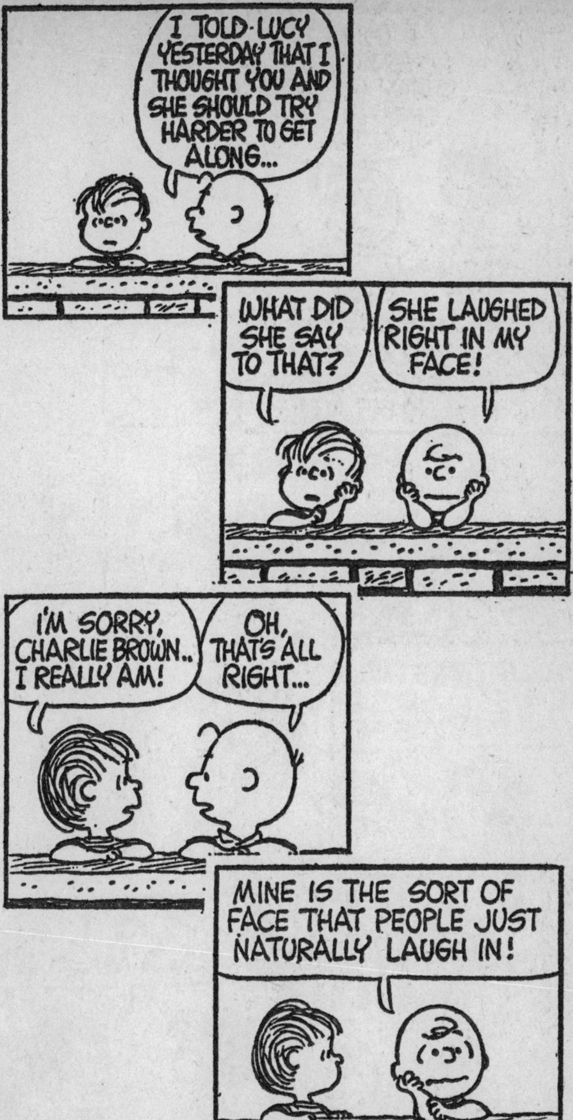
I TOLD LUCY YESTERDAY THAT I THOUGHT YOU AND SHE SHOULD TRY HARDER TO GET ALONG...
WHAT DID SHE SAY TO THAT?
SHE LAUGHED RIGHT IN MY FACE!
I'M SORRY, CHARLIE BROWN.. I REALLY AM!
OH, THAT'S ALL RIGHT...
MINE IS THE SORT OF FACE THAT PEOPLE JUST NATURALLY LAUGH IN!

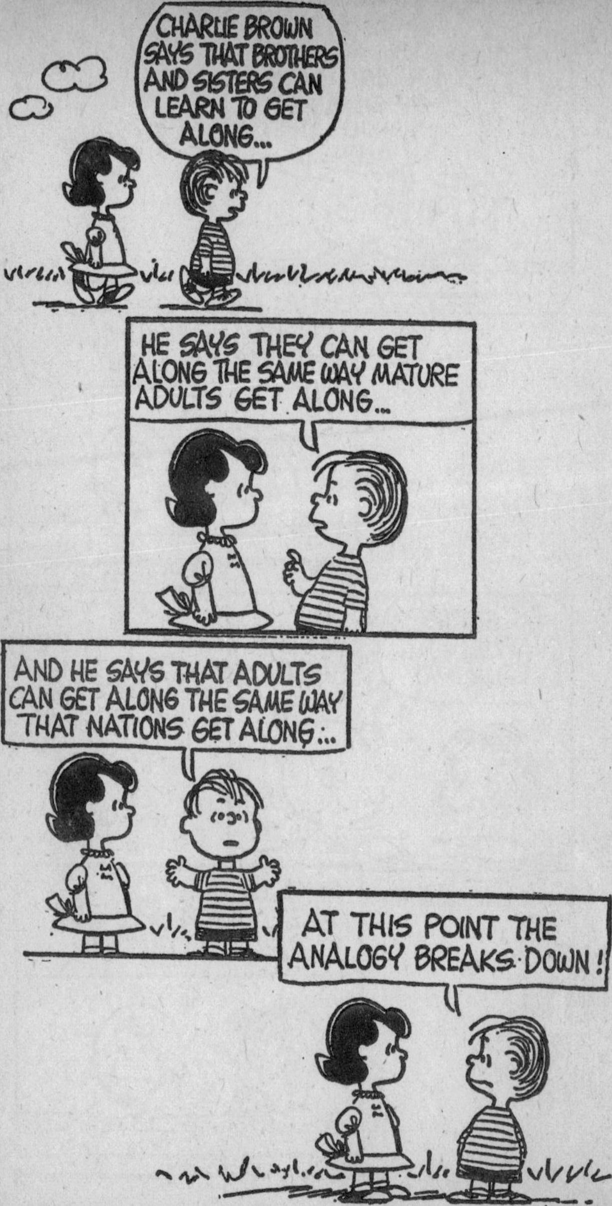
CHARLIE BROWN SAYS THAT BROTHERS AND SISTERS CAN LEARN TO GET ALONG...
HE SAYS THEY CAN GET ALONG THE SAME WAY MATURE ADULTS GET ALONG...
AND HE SAYS THAT ADULTS CAN GET ALONG THE SAME WAY THAT NATIONS GET ALONG...
AT THIS POINT THE ANALOGY BREAKS DOWN!

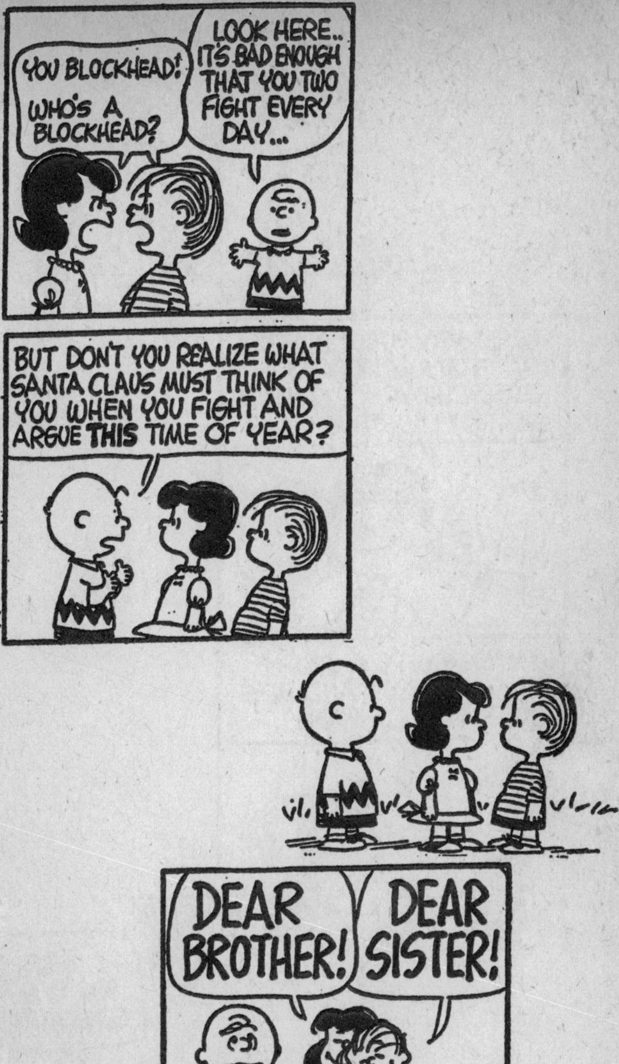
YOU BLOCKHEAD!
WHO'S A BLOCKHEAD?
LOOK HERE.. IT'S BAD ENOUGH THAT YOU TWO FIGHT EVERY DAY...
BUT DON'T YOU REALIZE WHAT SANTA CLAUS MUST THINK OF YOU WHEN YOU FIGHT AND ARGUE **THIS** TIME OF YEAR?
DEAR BROTHER!
DEAR SISTER!

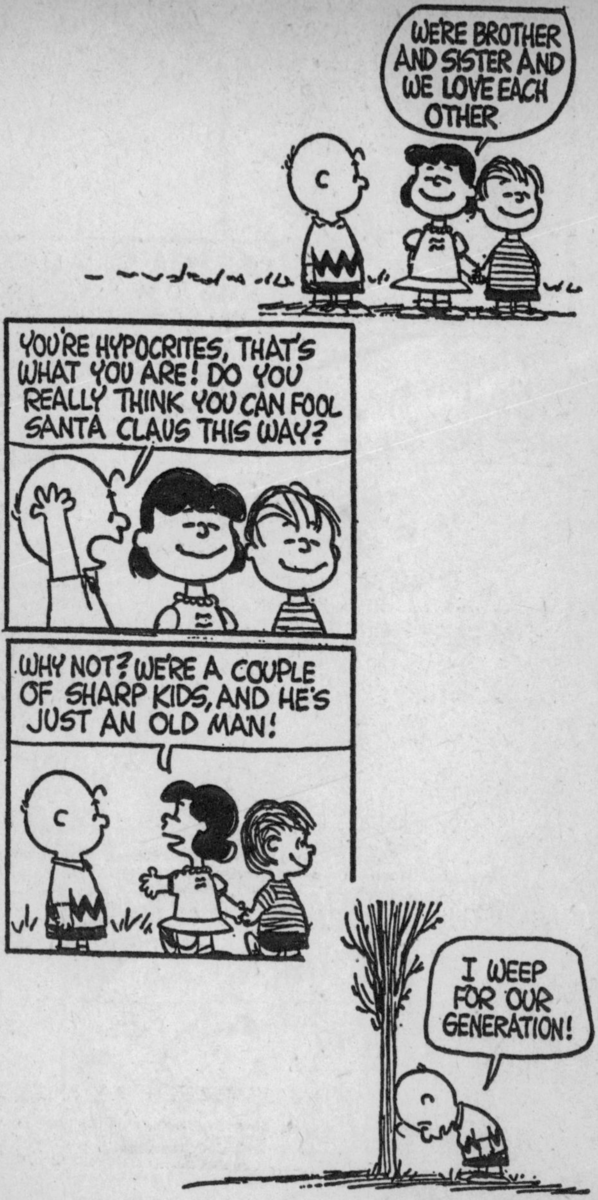

WE'RE BROTHER AND SISTER AND WE LOVE EACH OTHER
YOU'RE HYPOCRITES, THAT'S WHAT YOU ARE! DO YOU REALLY THINK YOU CAN FOOL SANTA CLAUS THIS WAY?
WHY NOT? WE'RE A COUPLE OF SHARP KIDS, AND HE'S JUST AN OLD MAN!
I WEEP FOR OUR GENERATION!

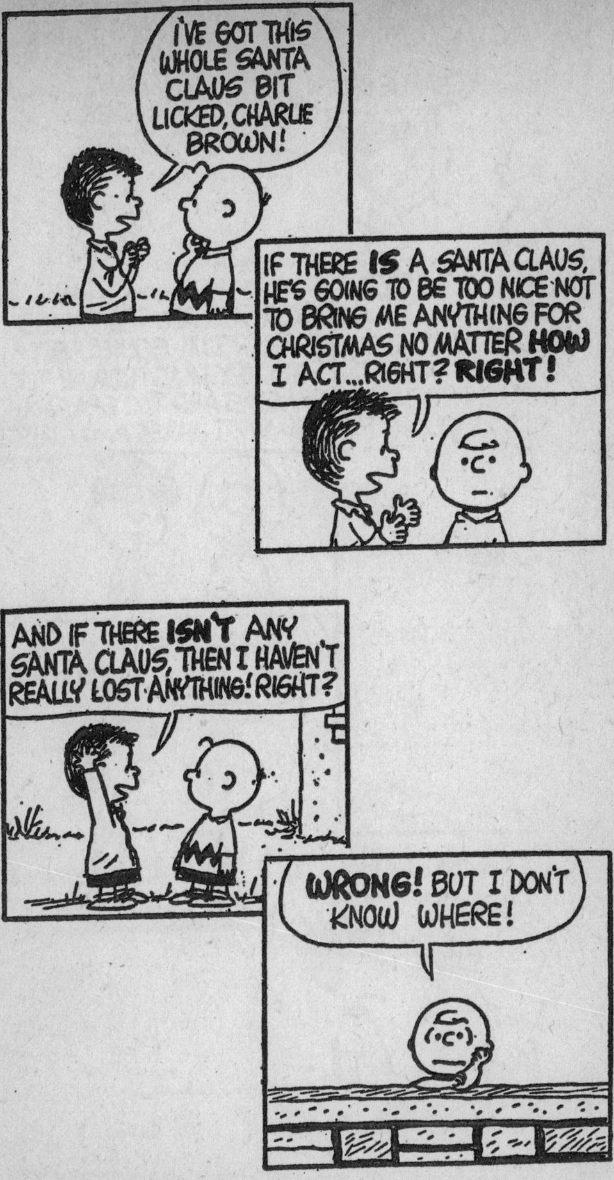
I'VE GOT THIS WHOLE SANTA CLAUS BIT LICKED, CHARLIE BROWN!
IF THERE IS A SANTA CLAUS, HE'S GOING TO BE TOO NICE NOT TO BRING ME ANYTHING FOR CHRISTMAS NO MATTER HOW I ACT...RIGHT? RIGHT!
AND IF THERE ISN'T ANY SANTA CLAUS, THEN I HAVEN'T REALLY LOST ANYTHING! RIGHT?
WRONG! BUT I DON'T KNOW WHERE!

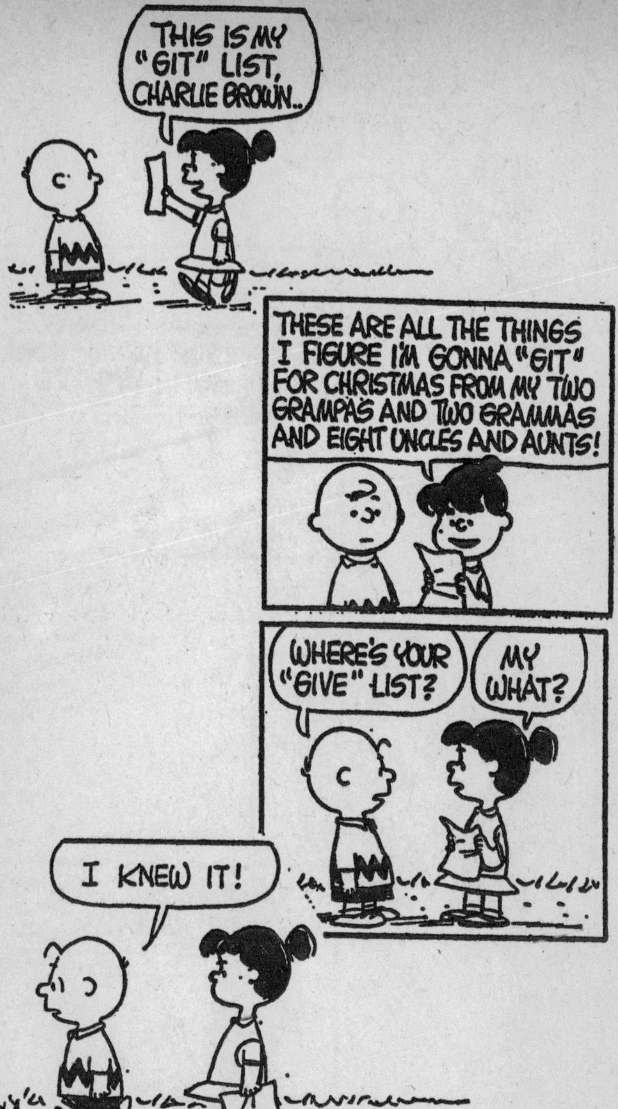

THIS IS MY "GIT" LIST, CHARLIE BROWN..
THESE ARE ALL THE THINGS I FIGURE I'M GONNA "GIT" FOR CHRISTMAS FROM MY TWO GRAMPA'S AND TWO GRAMMAS AND EIGHT UNCLES AND AUNTS!
WHERE'S YOUR "GIVE" LIST?
MY WHAT?
I KNEW IT!

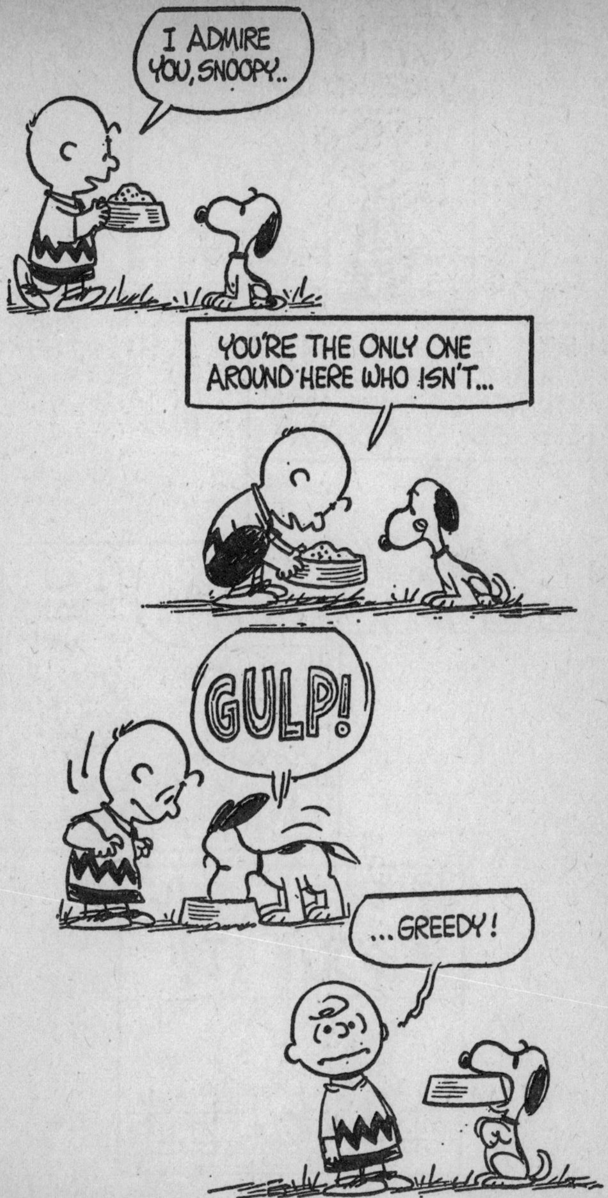
I ADMIRE YOU, SNOOPY..
YOU'RE THE ONLY ONE AROUND HERE WHO ISN'T...
GULP!
...GREEDY!

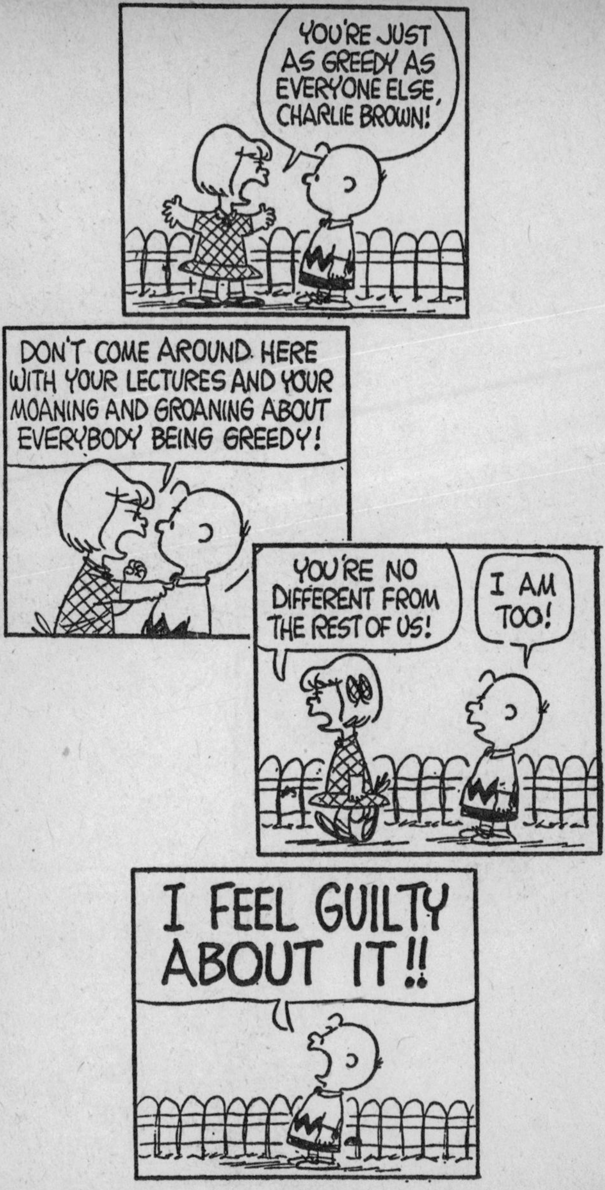
YOU'RE JUST AS GREEDY AS EVERYONE ELSE, CHARLIE BROWN!
DON'T COME AROUND HERE WITH YOUR LECTURES AND YOUR MOANING AND GROANING ABOUT EVERYBODY BEING GREEDY!
YOU'RE NO DIFFERENT FROM THE REST OF US!
I AM TOO!
I FEEL GUILTY ABOUT IT!!

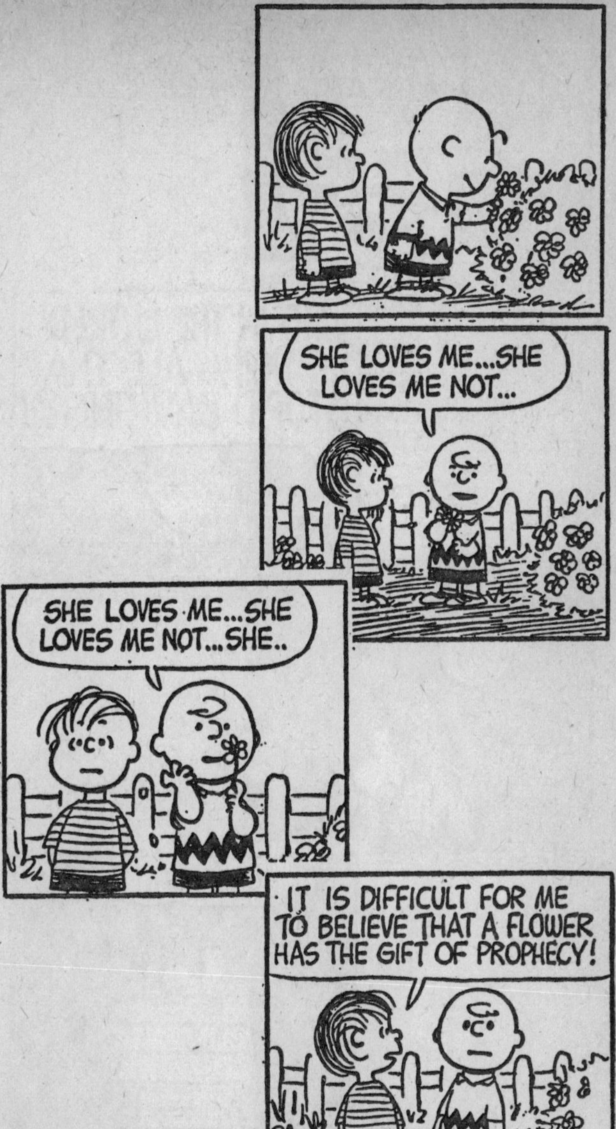
SHE LOVES ME...SHE LOVES ME NOT...
SHE LOVES ME...SHE LOVES ME NOT...SHE..
IT IS DIFFICULT FOR ME TO BELIEVE THAT A FLOWER HAS THE GIFT OF PROPHECY!

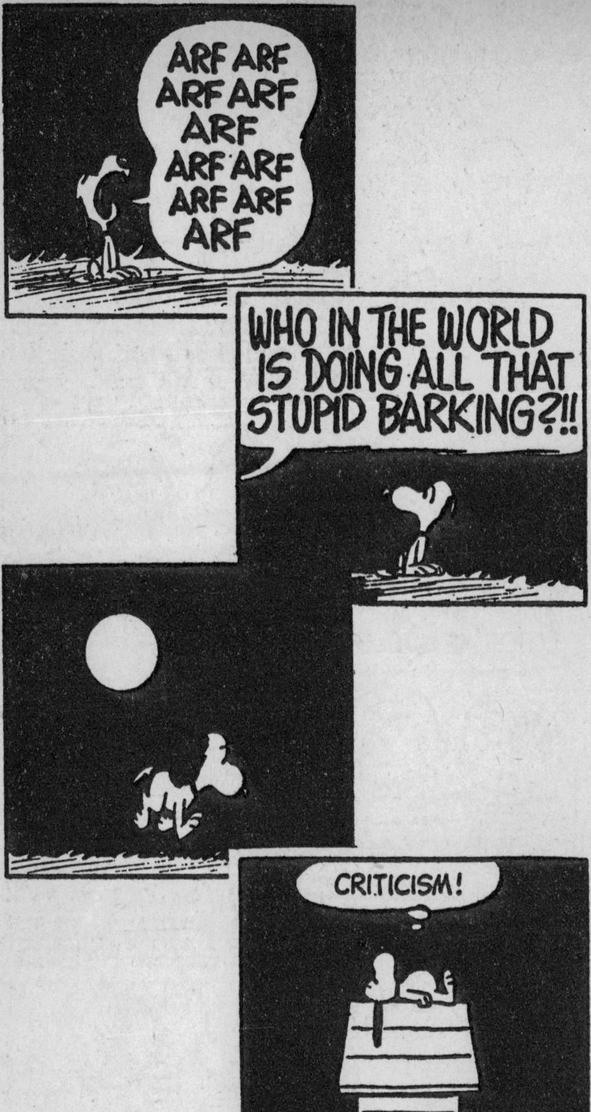
ARF ARF ARF ARF ARF ARF ARF ARF ARF ARF
WHO IN THE WORLD IS DOING ALL THAT STUPID BARKING?!!
CRITICISM!

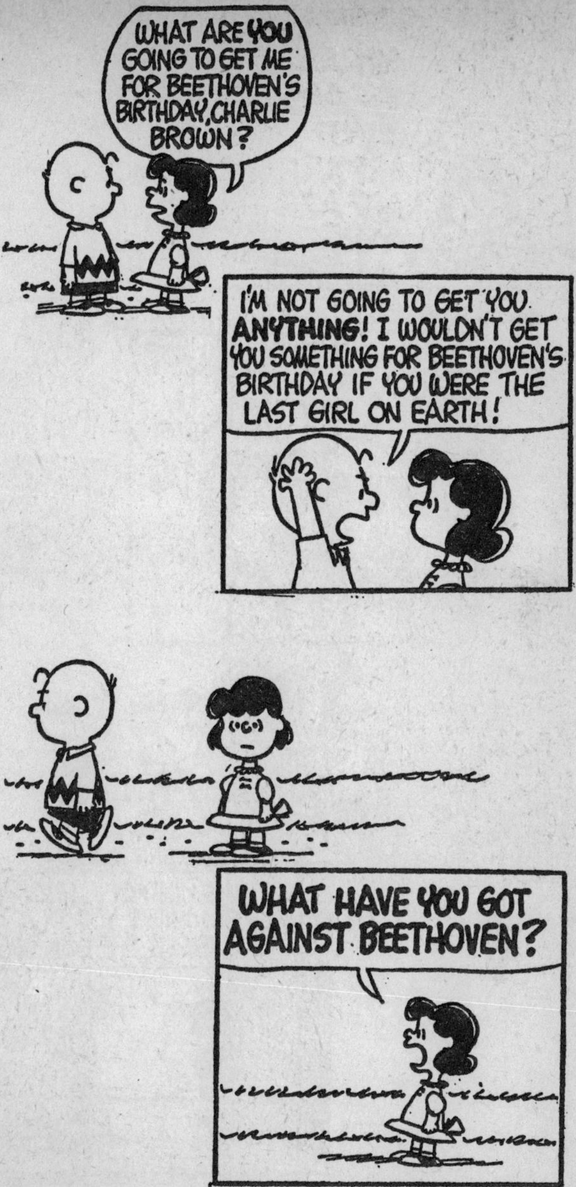
WHAT ARE YOU GOING TO GET ME FOR BEETHOVEN'S BIRTHDAY, CHARLIE BROWN?
I'M NOT GOING TO GET YOU ANYTHING! I WOULDN'T GET YOU SOMETHING FOR BEETHOVEN'S BIRTHDAY IF YOU WERE THE LAST GIRL ON EARTH!
WHAT HAVE YOU GOT AGAINST BEETHOVEN?

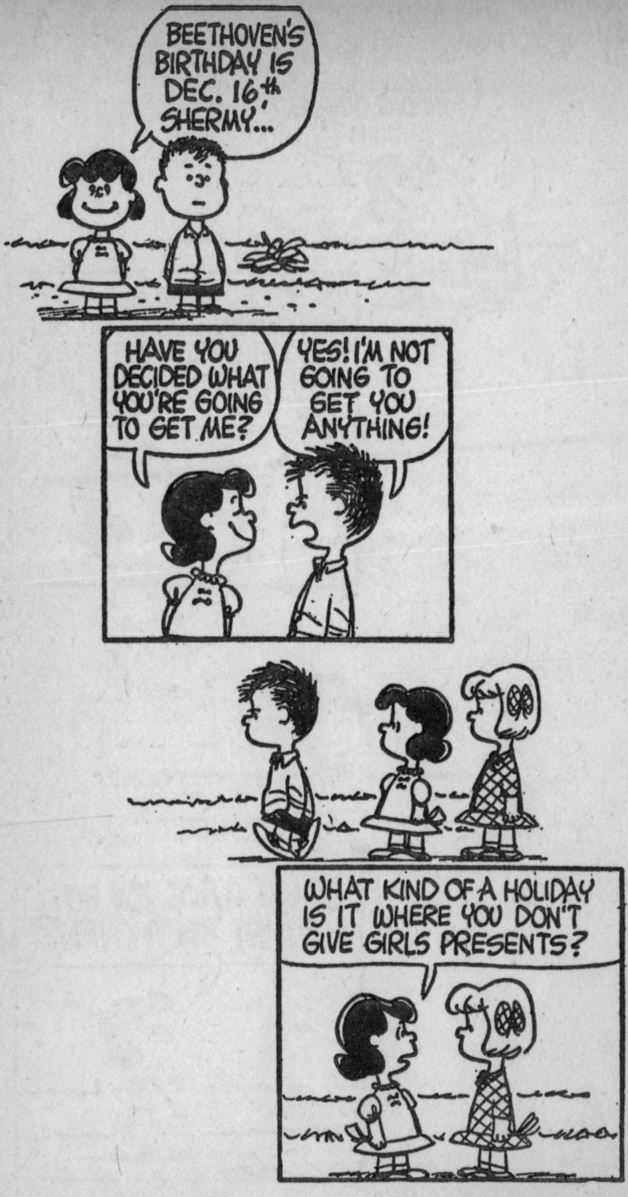
BEETHOVEN'S BIRTHDAY IS DEC. 16th SHERMY...
HAVE YOU DECIDED WHAT YOU'RE GOING TO GET ME?
YES! I'M NOT GOING TO GET YOU ANYTHING!
WHAT KIND OF A HOLIDAY IS IT WHERE YOU DON'T GIVE GIRLS PRESENTS?

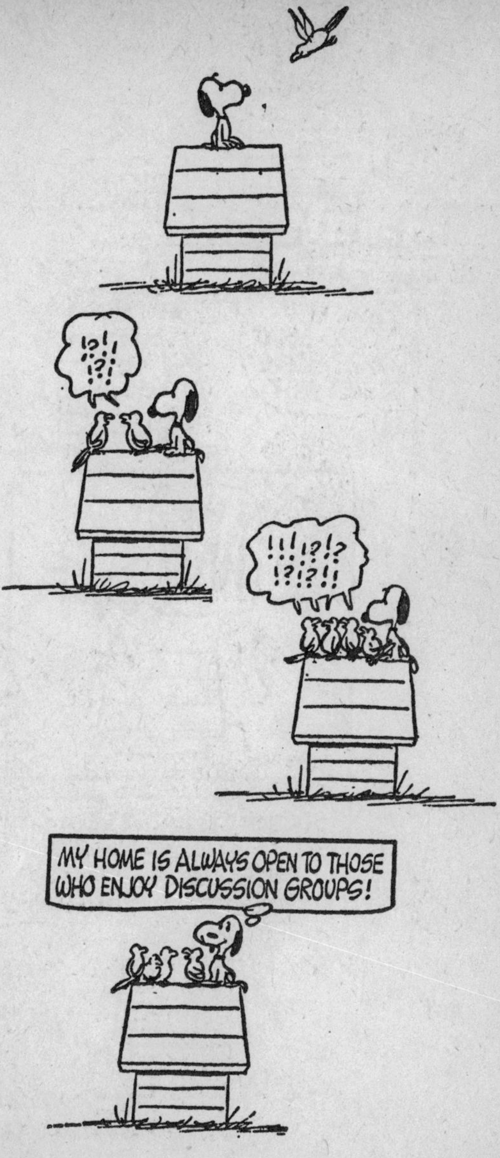
MY HOME IS ALWAYS OPEN TO THOSE WHO ENJOY DISCUSSION GROUPS!

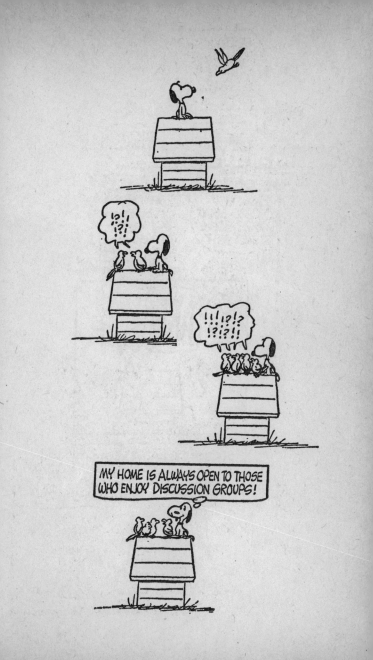

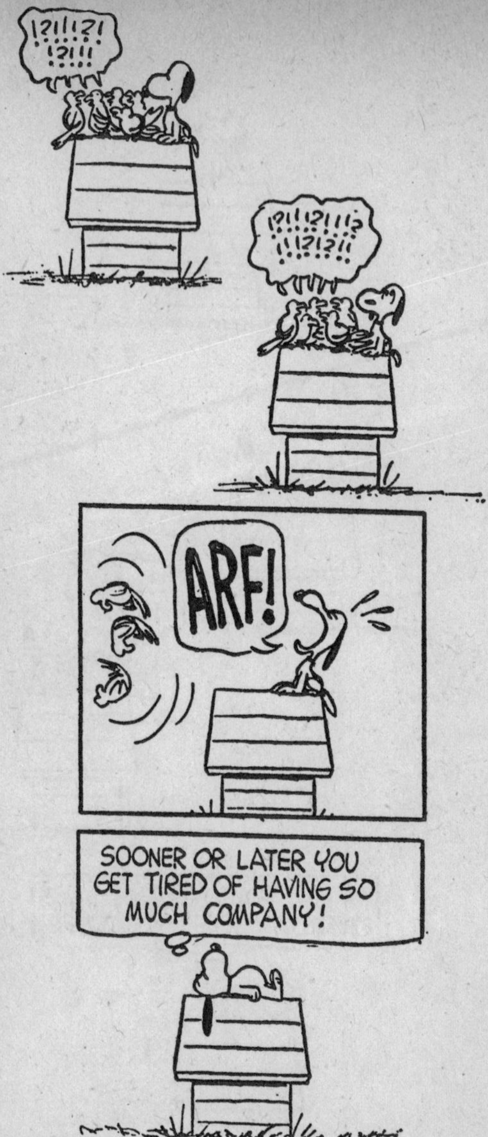
!?!!!?!
!?!!!
!?!!!?!!!?
!!!?!?!!
ARF!
SOONER OR LATER YOU GET TIRED OF HAVING SO MUCH COMPANY!

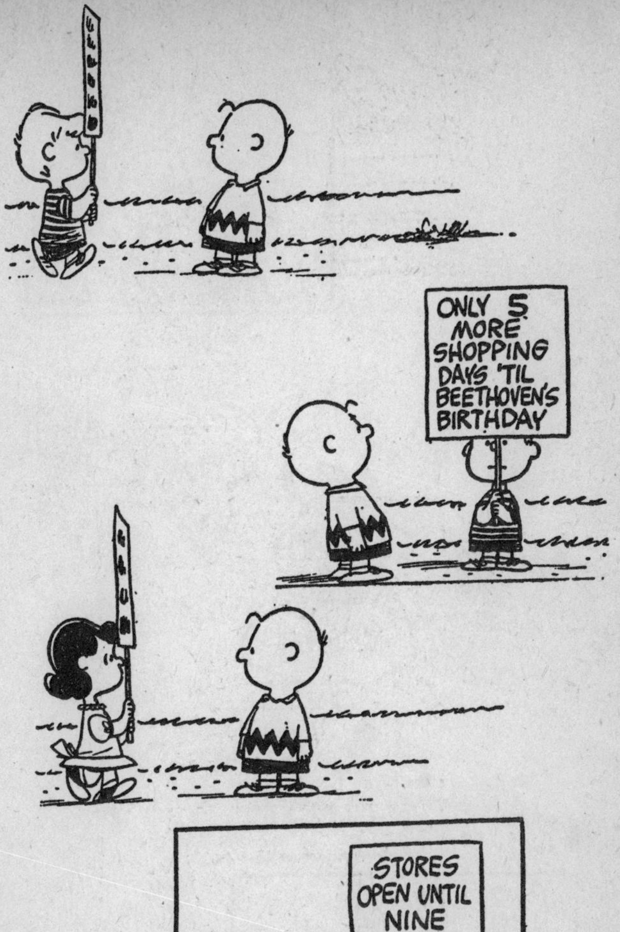
ONLY 5 MORE SHOPPING DAYS 'TIL BEETHOVEN'S BIRTHDAY
STORES OPEN UNTIL NINE O'CLOCK

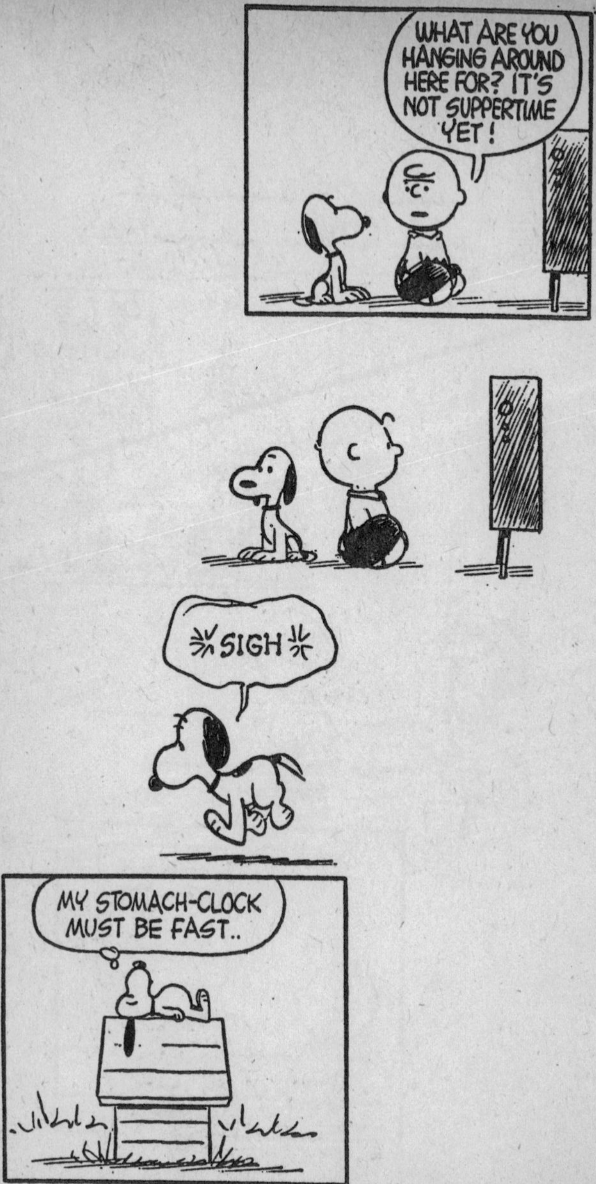
WHAT ARE YOU HANGING AROUND HERE FOR? IT'S NOT SUPPERTIME YET!
SIGH
MY STOMACH-CLOCK MUST BE FAST..

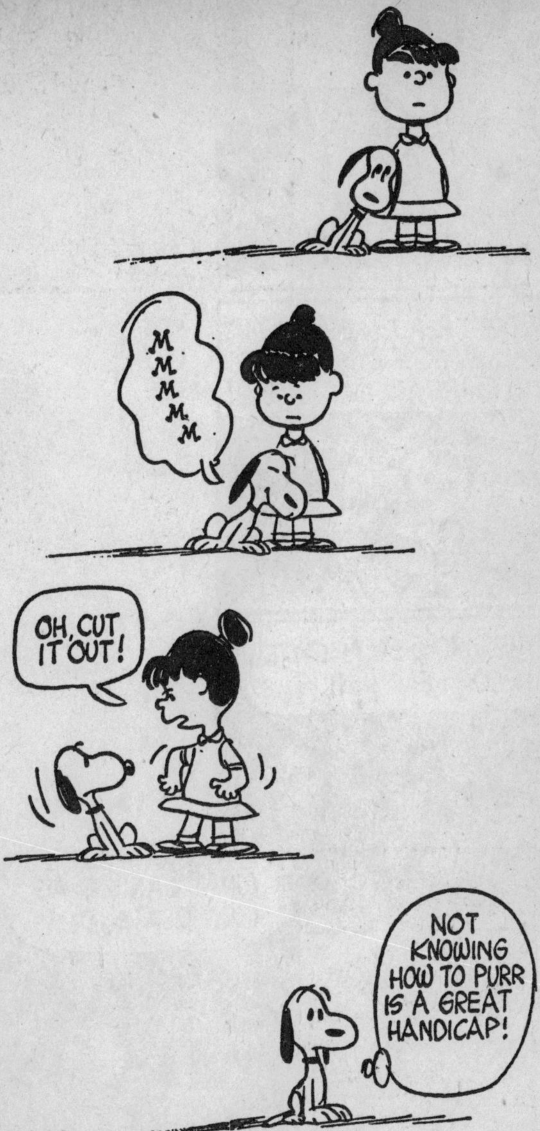
M M M M M
OH, CUT IT OUT!
NOT KNOWING HOW TO PURR IS A GREAT HANDICAP!

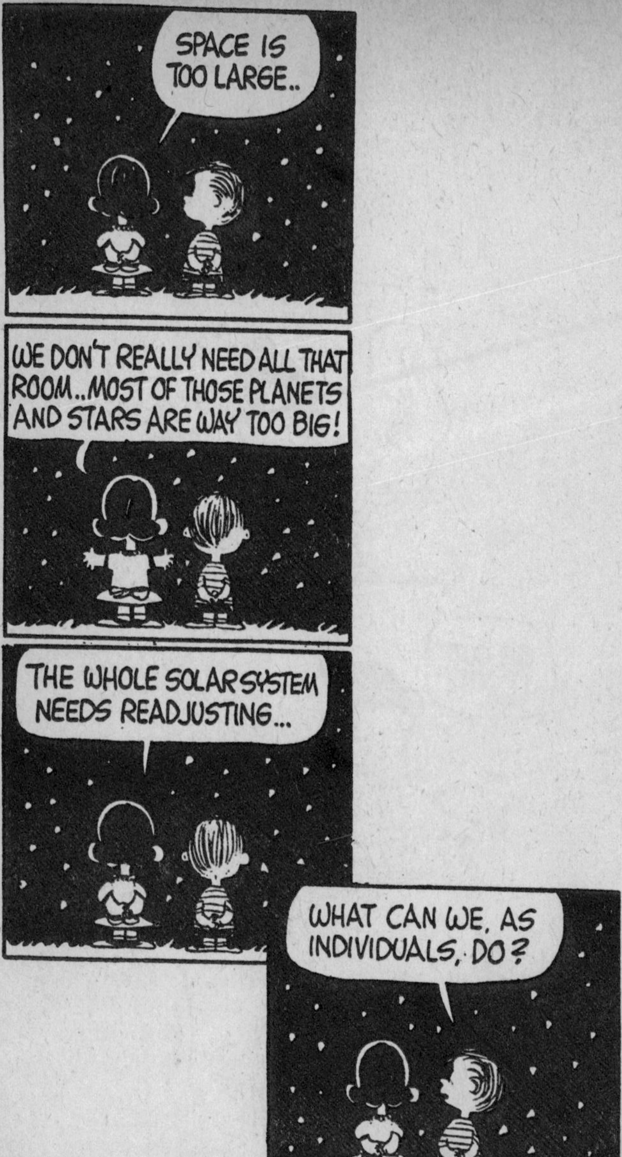

SPACE IS TOO LARGE..
WE DON'T REALLY NEED ALL THAT ROOM..MOST OF THOSE PLANETS AND STARS ARE WAY TOO BIG!
THE WHOLE SOLAR SYSTEM NEEDS READJUSTING...
WHAT CAN WE, AS INDIVIDUALS, DO?

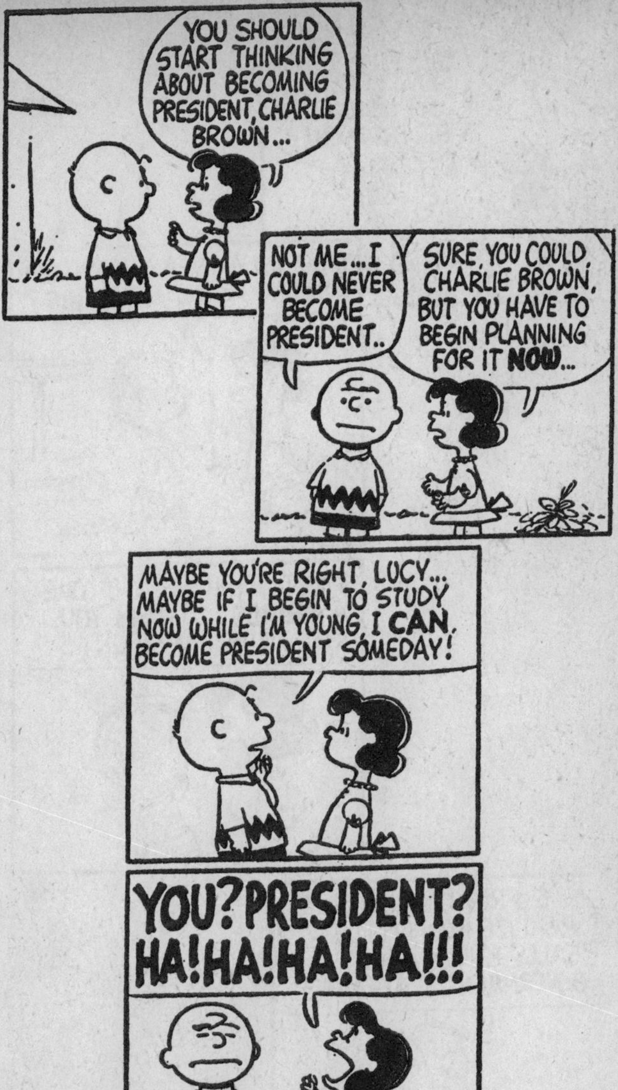
YOU SHOULD START THINKING ABOUT BECOMING PRESIDENT, CHARLIE BROWN...
NOT ME...I COULD NEVER BECOME PRESIDENT..
SURE, YOU COULD, CHARLIE BROWN, BUT YOU HAVE TO BEGIN PLANNING FOR IT **NOW**...
MAYBE YOU'RE RIGHT, LUCY... MAYBE IF I BEGIN TO STUDY NOW WHILE I'M YOUNG, I **CAN** BECOME PRESIDENT SOMEDAY!
YOU? PRESIDENT? HA! HA! HA! HA!!!

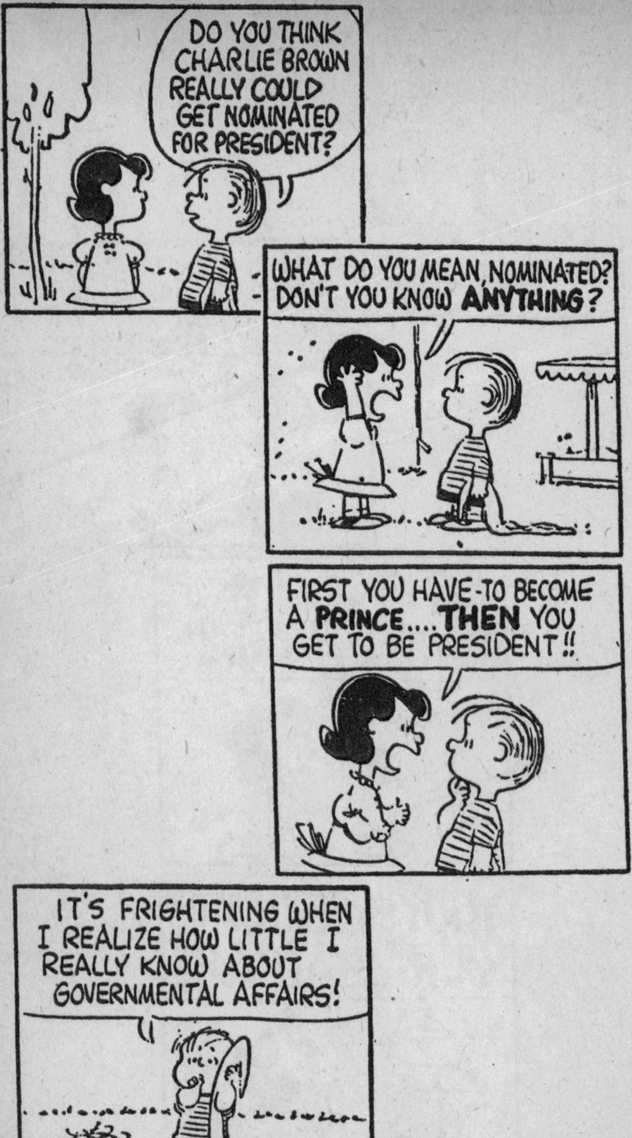
DO YOU THINK CHARLIE BROWN REALLY COULD GET NOMINATED FOR PRESIDENT?
WHAT DO YOU MEAN, NOMINATED? DON'T YOU KNOW ANYTHING?
FIRST YOU HAVE-TO BECOME A PRINCE....THEN YOU GET TO BE PRESIDENT!!
IT'S FRIGHTENING WHEN I REALIZE HOW LITTLE I REALLY KNOW ABOUT GOVERNMENTAL AFFAIRS!

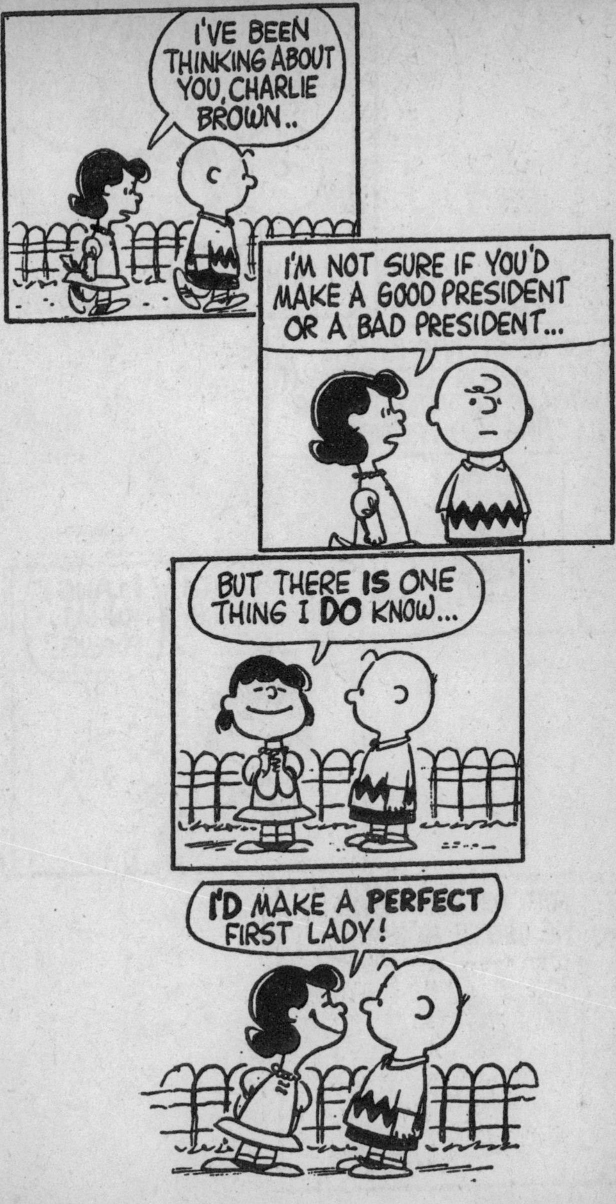
I'VE BEEN THINKING ABOUT YOU, CHARLIE BROWN..
I'M NOT SURE IF YOU'D MAKE A GOOD PRESIDENT OR A BAD PRESIDENT...
BUT THERE **IS** ONE THING I **DO** KNOW...
I'D MAKE A **PERFECT** FIRST LADY!

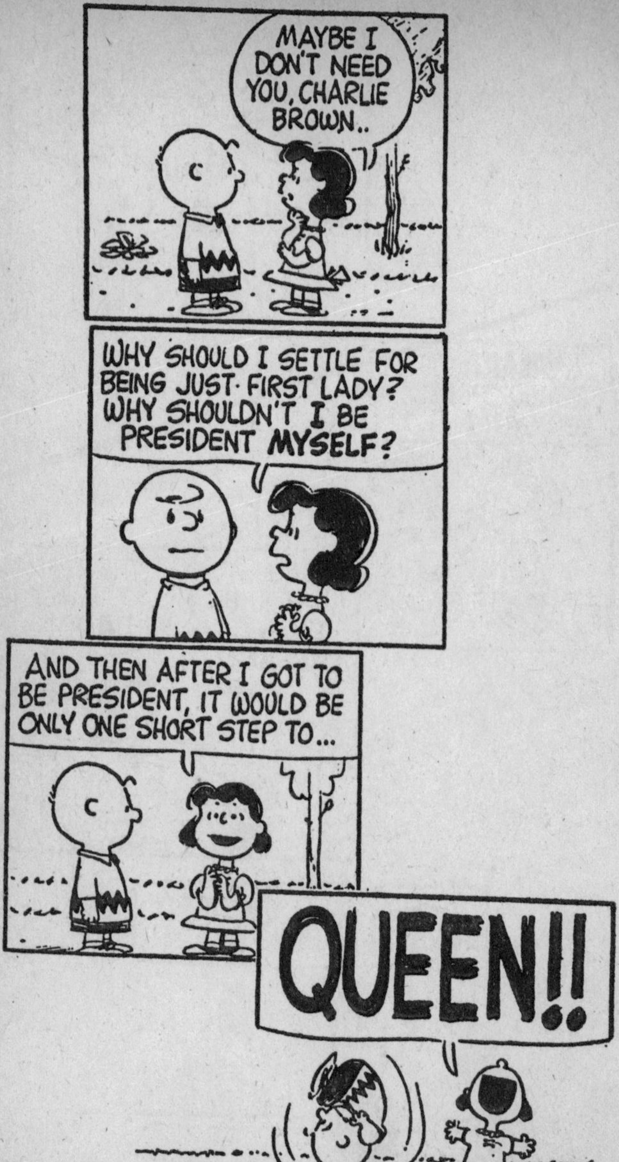
MAYBE I DON'T NEED YOU, CHARLIE BROWN..
WHY SHOULD I SETTLE FOR BEING JUST FIRST LADY? WHY SHOULDN'T I BE PRESIDENT MYSELF?
AND THEN AFTER I GOT TO BE PRESIDENT, IT WOULD BE ONLY ONE SHORT STEP TO...
QUEEN!!

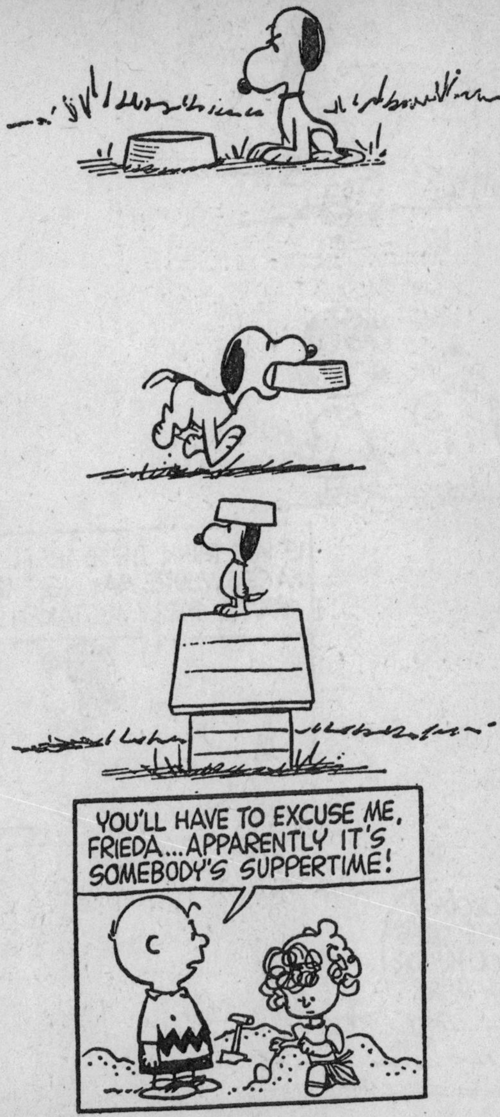
YOU'LL HAVE TO EXCUSE ME, FRIEDA....APPARENTLY IT'S SOMEBODY'S SUPPERTIME!

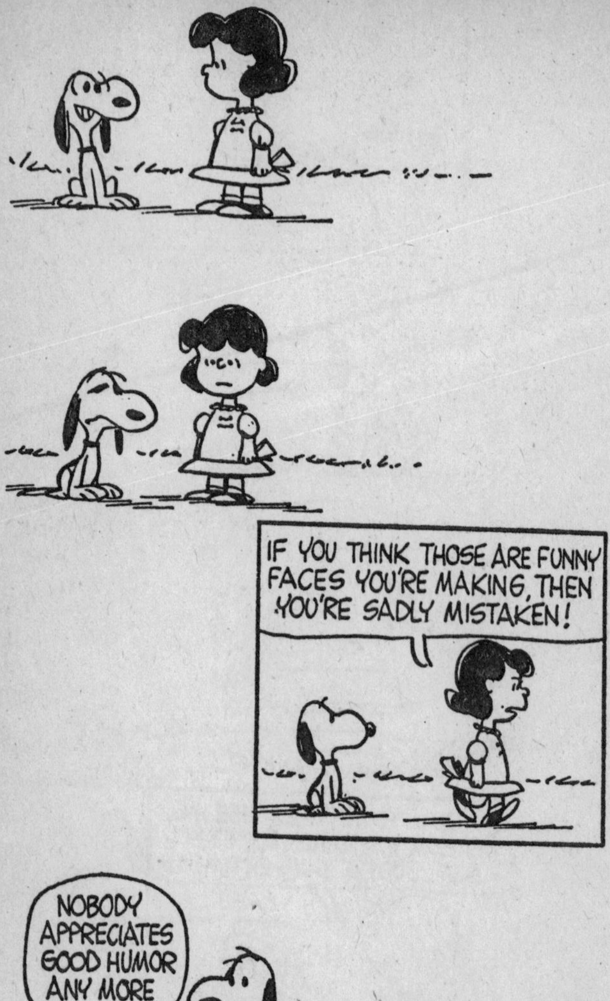
IF YOU THINK THOSE ARE FUNNY FACES YOU'RE MAKING, THEN YOU'RE SADLY MISTAKEN!
NOBODY APPRECIATES GOOD HUMOR ANY MORE

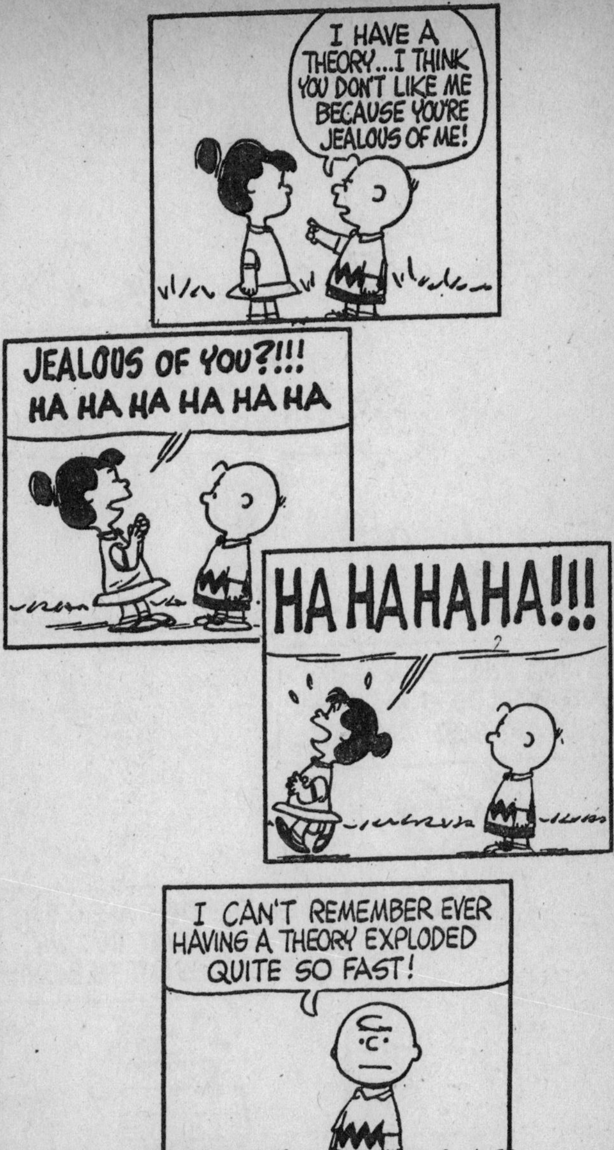
I HAVE A THEORY...I THINK YOU DON'T LIKE ME BECAUSE YOU'RE JEALOUS OF ME!
JEALOUS OF YOU?!!! HA HA HA HA HA HA
HA HA HA HA!!!
I CAN'T REMEMBER EVER HAVING A THEORY EXPLODED QUITE SO FAST!

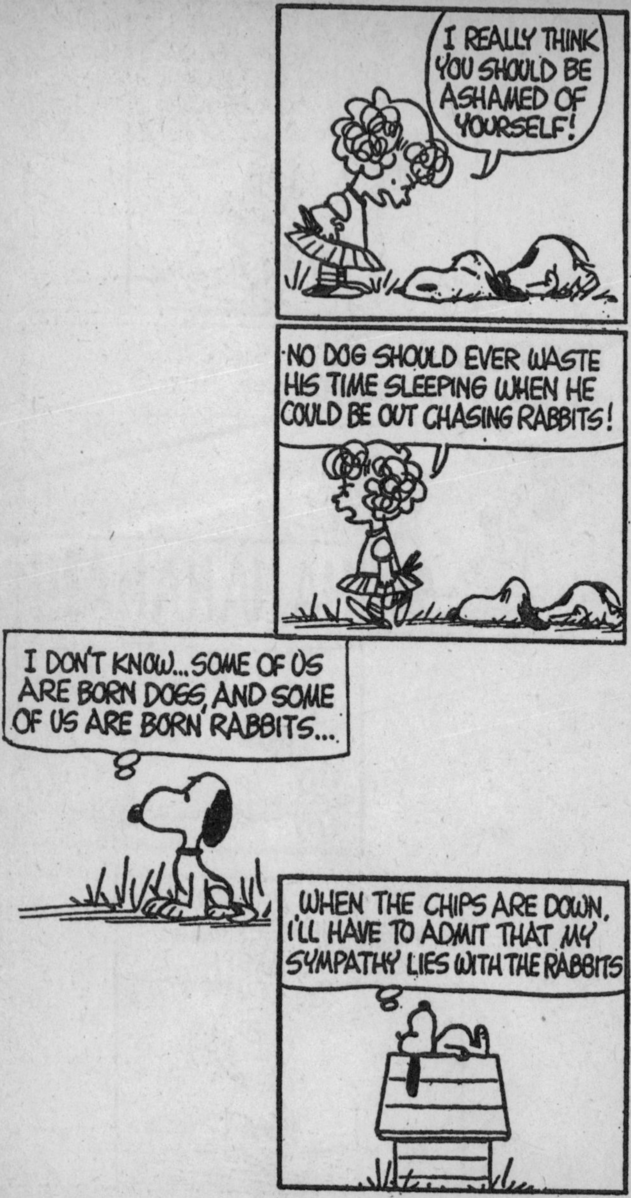
I REALLY THINK YOU SHOULD BE ASHAMED OF YOURSELF!
NO DOG SHOULD EVER WASTE HIS TIME SLEEPING WHEN HE COULD BE OUT CHASING RABBITS!
I DON'T KNOW...SOME OF US ARE BORN DOGS, AND SOME OF US ARE BORN RABBITS...
WHEN THE CHIPS ARE DOWN, I'LL HAVE TO ADMIT THAT MY SYMPATHY LIES WITH THE RABBITS

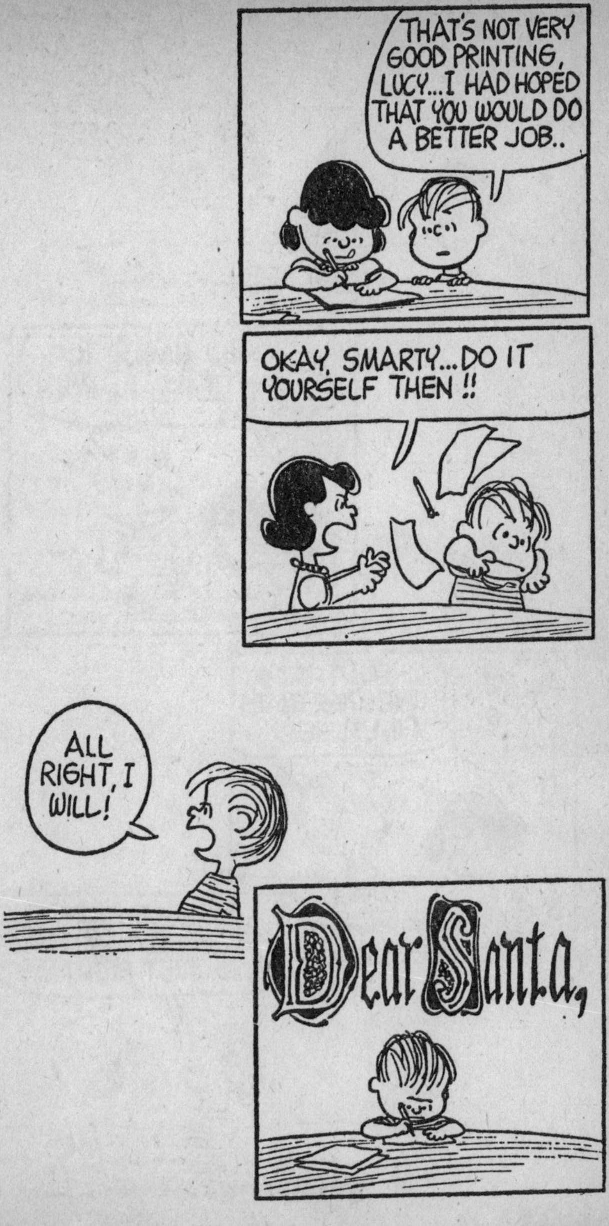
THAT'S NOT VERY GOOD PRINTING, LUCY...I HAD HOPED THAT YOU WOULD DO A BETTER JOB..
OKAY, SMARTY...DO IT YOURSELF THEN !!
ALL RIGHT, I WILL!
Dear Santa,

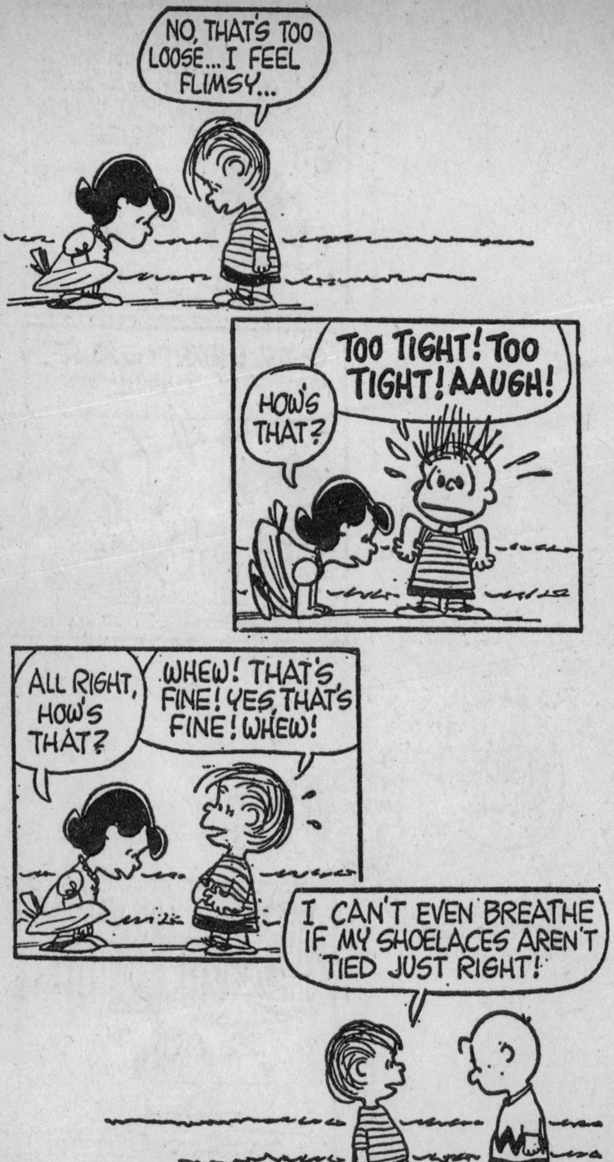

NO, THAT'S TOO LOOSE...I FEEL FLIMSY...
HOW'S THAT?
TOO TIGHT! TOO TIGHT! AAUGH!
ALL RIGHT, HOW'S THAT?
WHEW! THAT'S FINE! YES, THAT'S FINE! WHEW!
I CAN'T EVEN BREATHE IF MY SHOELACES AREN'T TIED JUST RIGHT!

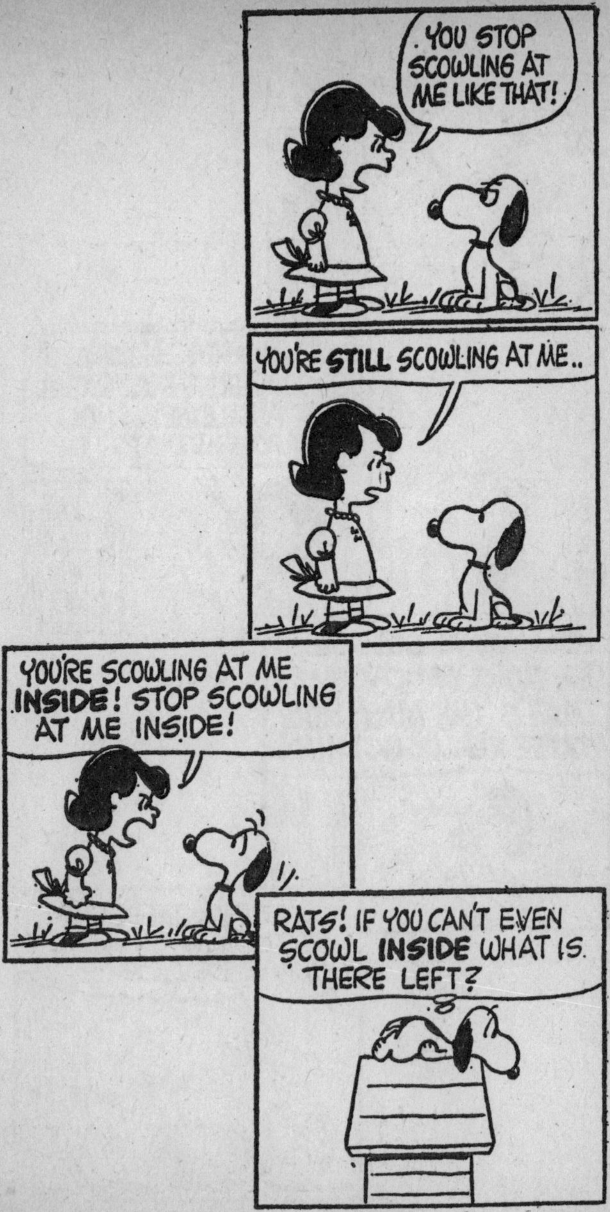
YOU STOP SCOWLING AT ME LIKE THAT!
YOU'RE **STILL** SCOWLING AT ME..
YOU'RE SCOWLING AT ME **INSIDE**! STOP SCOWLING AT ME INSIDE!
RATS! IF YOU CAN'T EVEN SCOWL **INSIDE** WHAT IS THERE LEFT?

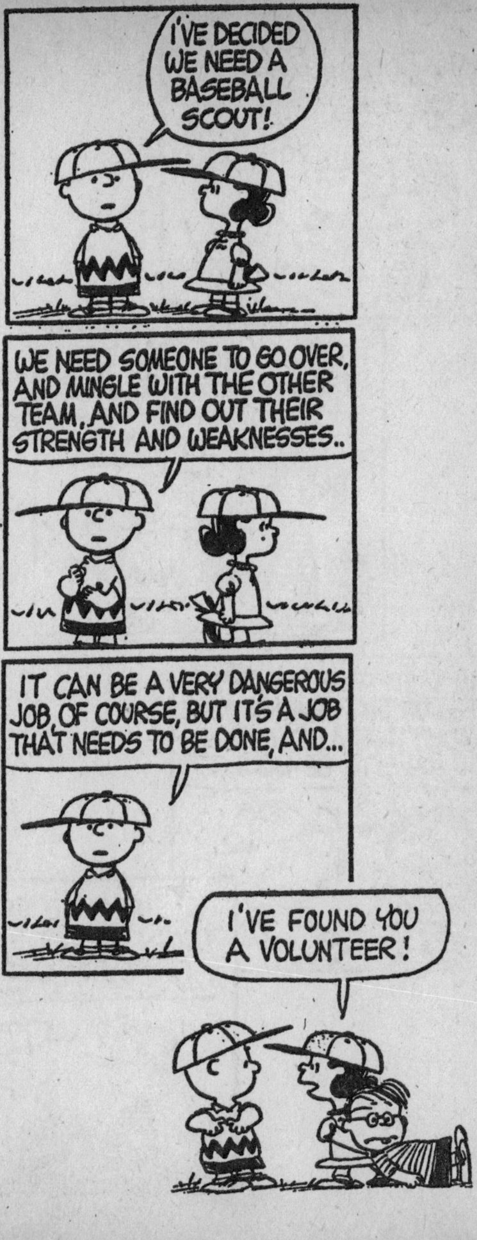
I'VE DECIDED WE NEED A BASEBALL SCOUT!
WE NEED SOMEONE TO GO OVER, AND MINGLE WITH THE OTHER TEAM, AND FIND OUT THEIR STRENGTH AND WEAKNESSES..
IT CAN BE A VERY DANGEROUS JOB, OF COURSE, BUT IT'S A JOB THAT NEEDS TO BE DONE, AND...
I'VE FOUND YOU A VOLUNTEER!

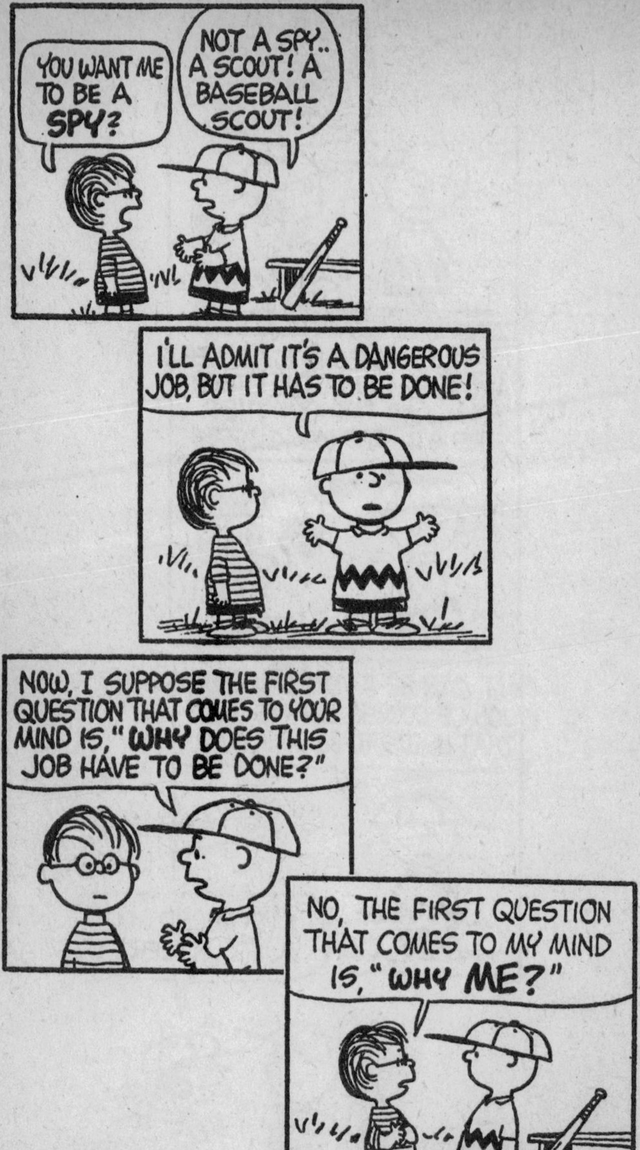
YOU WANT ME TO BE A SPY?
NOT A SPY.. A SCOUT! A BASEBALL SCOUT!
I'LL ADMIT IT'S A DANGEROUS JOB, BUT IT HAS TO BE DONE!
NOW, I SUPPOSE THE FIRST QUESTION THAT COMES TO YOUR MIND IS, "WHY DOES THIS JOB HAVE TO BE DONE?"
NO, THE FIRST QUESTION THAT COMES TO MY MIND IS, "WHY ME?"

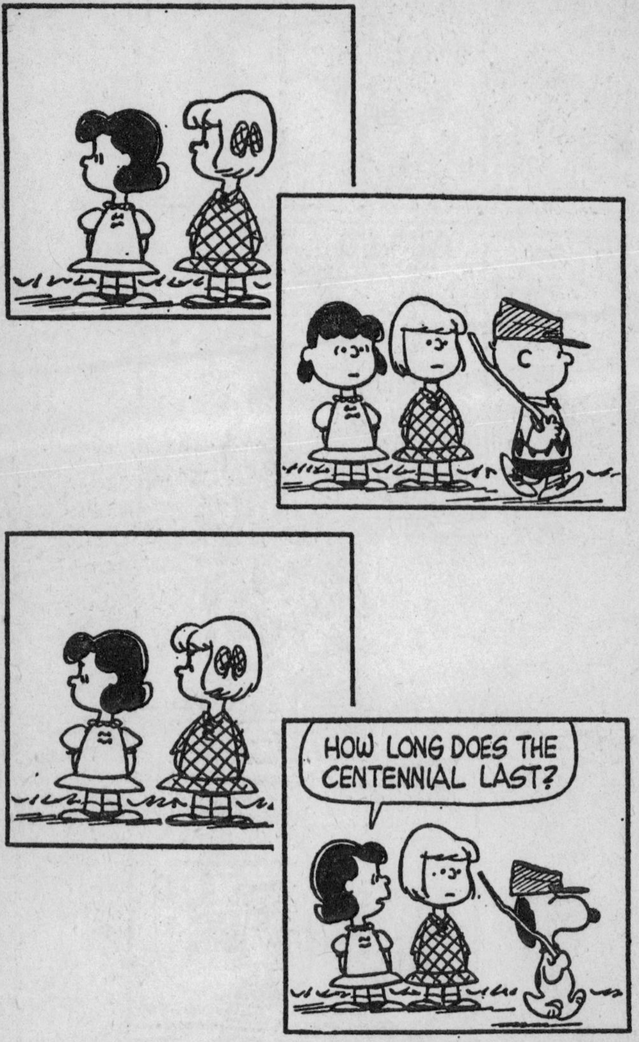
HOW LONG DOES THE CENTENNIAL LAST?

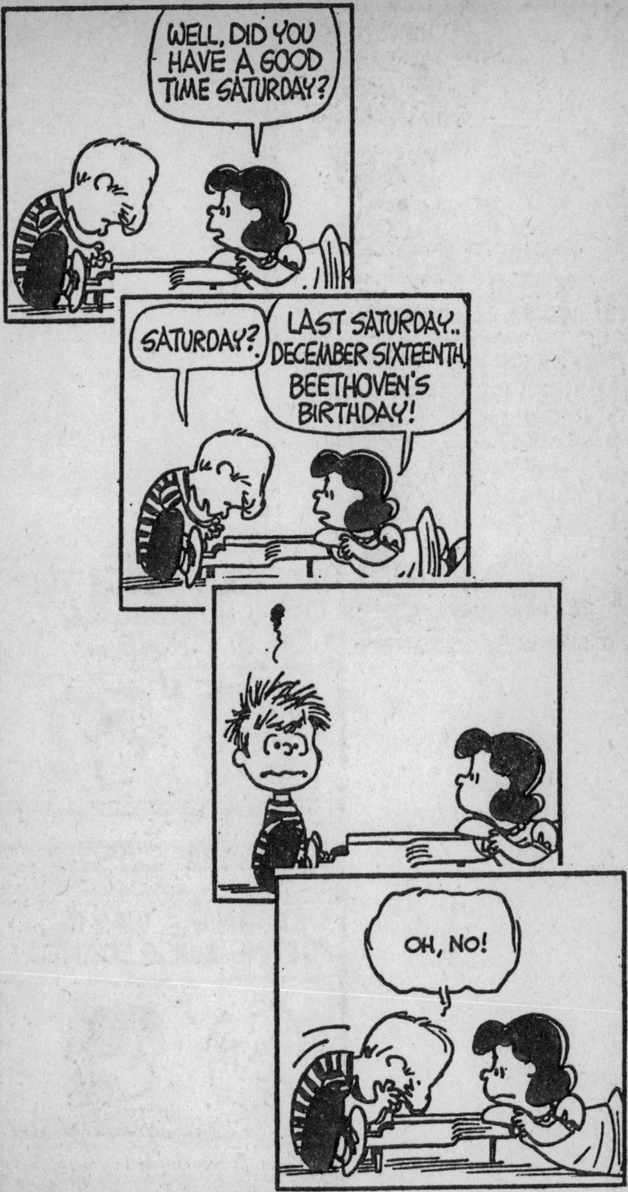
WELL, DID YOU HAVE A GOOD TIME SATURDAY?
SATURDAY?
LAST SATURDAY.. DECEMBER SIXTEENTH, BEETHOVEN'S BIRTHDAY!
OH, NO!

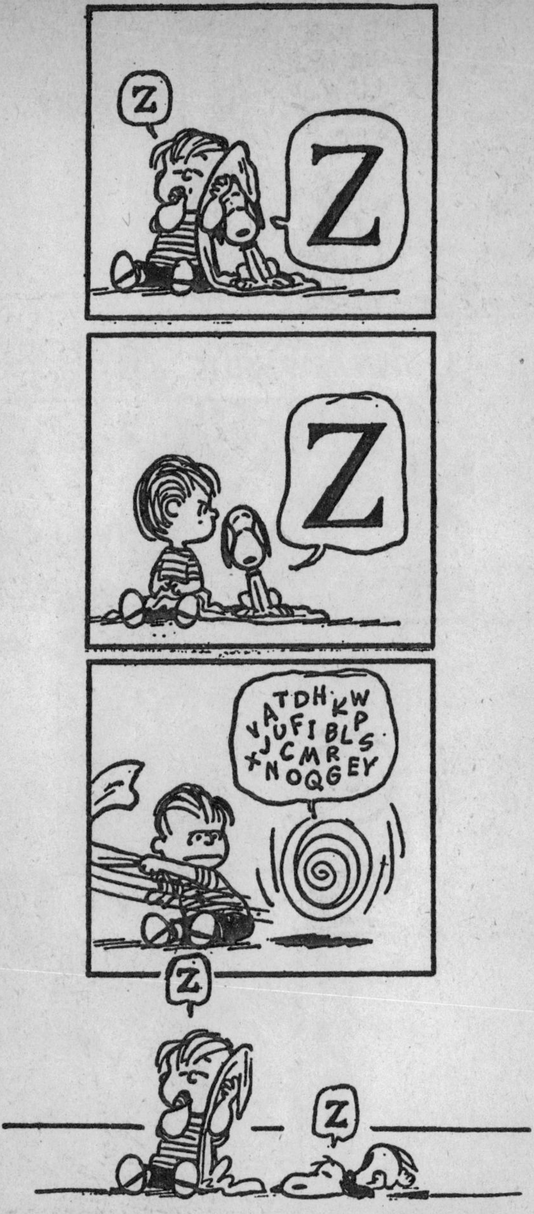
Z
Z
Z
ATDH KW
VA UFI BL P
J CMR S
X NOQGEY
Z
Z

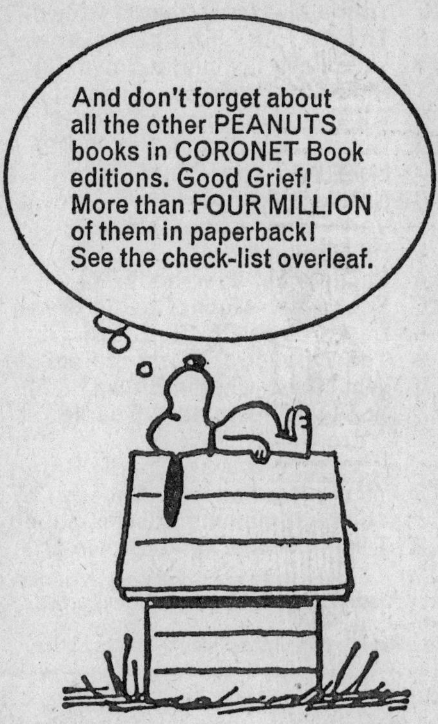
And don't forget about
all the other PEANUTS
books in CORONET Book
editions. Good Grief!
More than FOUR MILLION
of them in paperback!
See the check-list overleaf.

Wherever Paperbacks Are Sold

FOR THE LOVE OF PEANUTS

☐	02710 X	For The Love of Peanuts (2)	50p
☐	04491 8	Good Ol' Snoopy (3)	50p
☐	04409 8	Who Do You Think You Are, Charlie Brown (4)	50p
☐	04305 9	Fun With Peanuts (5)	50p
☐	04295 8	Here Comes Snoopy (6)	50p
☐	04318 0	You're My Hero, Charlie Brown (7)	50p
☐	04406 3	This Is Your Life, Charlie Brown (8)	50p
☐	04294 X	Let's Face It, Charlie Brown (9)	50p
☐	04407 1	Slide Charlie Brown, Slide (10)	50p
☐	04405 5	All This And Snoopy Too (11)	50p
☐	10788 X	Good Grief, Charlie Brown (12)	50p
☐	10595 X	Here's To You, Charlie Brown (13)	50p
☐	10541 0	Nobody's Perfect Charlie Brown (14)	50p
☐	10673 5	Very Funny, Charlie Brown (15)	50p
☐	10761 8	Hey, Peanuts (17)	50p
☐	12609 4	Peanuts For Everybody (20)	50p
☐	12614 0	You're Too Much, Charlie Brown (21)	50p
☐	12618 3	Here Comes Charlie Brown (22)	50p
☐	12543 8	The Wonderful World of Peanuts (24)	50p
☐	12544 6	What Next, Charlie Brown? (26)	50p
☐	15135 8	You're The Greatest, Charlie Brown (27)	50p
☐	15828 X	Have It Your Way, Charlie Brown (29)	50p
☐	15698 8	You're Not For Real, Snoopy (30)	50p
☐	17322 X	You're Something Special, Snoopy (33)	50p
☐	17844 2	Take It Easy, Charlie Brown (35)	50p

All these books are available at your local bookshop or newsagent, or can be ordered direct from the publisher. Just tick the titles you want and fill in the form below.

Prices and availability subject to change without notice.

~~~~~~

TEACH YOURSELF BOOKS, P.O. Box 11, Falmouth, Cornwall.

Please send cheque or postal order, and allow the following for postage and packing:

U.K. – One book 22p plus 10p per copy for each additional book ordered, up to a maximum of 82p.

B.F.P.O. and EIRE – 22p for the first book plus 10p per copy for the next 6 books, thereafter 4p per book.

OTHER OVERSEAS CUSTOMERS – 30p for the first book and 10p per copy for each additional book.

Name ....

Address ....

....